FENG SHUI
FOR
SKEPTICS

FENG SHUI
FOR
SKEPTICS

Real Solutions
Without Superstition

KARTAR DIAMOND

Four Pillars Publishing
CULVER CITY, CALIFORNIA

© 2004 Kartar Diamond. Printed and bound in the United States of America. All rights reserved. No part of this book may be reproduced or transmitted in any form or by any means, electronic or mechanical, including photocopying, recording, or by an information storage and retrieval system—except by a reviewer who may quote brief passages in a review to be printed in a magazine, newspaper, or on the Web—without permission in writing from the publisher. For information, please contact Four Pillars Publishing, 3824 Perham Drive, Culver City, CA 90232.

Although the author and publisher have made every effort to ensure the accuracy and completeness of information contained in this book, we assume no responsibility for errors, inaccuracies, omissions, or any inconsistency herein. Any slights of people, places, or organizations are unintentional.

First printing 2004
Second printing 2005

ISBN 0-9671937-8-8
LCCN 2003105373

ATTENTION CORPORATIONS, UNIVERSITIES, COLLEGES, AND PROFESSIONAL ORGANIZATIONS: Quantity discounts are available on bulk purchases of this book for educational, gift purposes, or as premiums for increasing magazine subscriptions or renewals. Special books or book excerpts can also be created to fit specific needs. For information, please contact Four Pillars Publishing, 3824 Perham Drive, Culver City, CA 90232; 310-842-8870.

This book is dedicated to two people...

Thank you, Master Sang,
for teaching me authentic feng shui
and always encouraging me to
teach, write and consult.

Thank you also to my son Nirangkar
for inspiring me to achieve my goals,
so that you will be proud
of your mom.

TABLE OF CONTENTS

INTRODUCTION

Feng shui, pronounced "fung shway," is a challenging topic to write about, unless one has a long-term plan to publish an encyclopedia to cover the subject properly. And yet, the basic concept that you are affected by your environment in non-obvious ways, is almost universally understood and initially appears quite simple and straightforward.

Feng shui theory's complicated and subtle explanations as to how and why we are affected seem preposterous to many—certainly not yet validated by any Western scientific measures. Thankfully, I don't feel it is necessary for the whole world to agree with me, or for them to seek me out, in order to feel the satisfaction I do in helping my clients. Once upon a time, I was a devout vegetarian and it didn't bother me at all that my beliefs were in the minority.

What surprises me to this day is how accepting the public has become of feng shui. It seems to have become almost mainstream. When I first started learning it, I could not have imagined consulting as a full-time career, nor hearing it discussed on CBS Nightly News (Connie Chung in January, 1995).

The downside of feng shui having become so popular is it has simply been diluted, convoluted and reinvented for mass consumption. Thus, the main urge for me to write this book is twofold: 1) to dispel the nonsense being passed off as feng shui, and 2) to actually deliver advanced but practical information without expecting the reader to abandon his or her current occupation in order to study feng shui full-time.

What I have seen in the vast majority of feng shui books is an emphasis on superstition or on general concepts that are not easily applied

1

to everyone. Readers who are hungry for feng shui knowledge end up obsessing over big generalities or minor details, while the uniqueness of their own environment remains a mystery. *Feng Shui for Skeptics* will answer some personal questions for thousands of readers when they see their own home or place of business described in these pages. My only other advice is to *not* read this book while driving or operating heavy machinery. Enjoy!

CHAPTER ONE

GROUND RULES

The world is definitely flat. At least, that is my impression when I stand outside and look as far and wide as my eyes can see. Of course, we know the earth is actually round. My point? How very limited our lives would be if we relied solely on what we can prove with only our five senses, not allowing for the fact that powerful energies and truths exist, even though they are not physically obvious. What, for that matter, does love "look" like?

Feng shui is the non-obvious reality of our environment. It is a phenomenon of this world and perhaps other planets as well. Feng literally means "wind" and shui literally means "water." It is an abbreviation of a whole concept: energy, dissipated by wind, collects at the boundaries of water. We are affected by things we cannot hear, see, smell, touch or taste. And yet, our five senses are very much involved in the experiences of any given environment. We are affected physically, emotionally, socially and even financially by non-obvious forces.

This book will not go into great detail about the history of feng shui, although there are indications its theories and practices have been around for more than 6,000 years. Neither will I be trying to prove by Western scientific standards that feng shui is a science. I do believe, some time in the future it will be validated by science. Until then, I prefer to call feng shui a near-science because it appears to have very

3

reliable, predictable outcomes or effects on people when environments and circumstances are similar. Certain house types will almost always have the same effects on whatever type of person occupies the dwelling. I say "almost" because it is nearly impossible to predict or expect an identical outcome, since there are so many other variables to consider.

For example, compare two houses built in the same year, facing the same direction and with the same floor plan. Although the two houses are similar, if there are different people living in them, with different furnishings, using the space differently, they will have different experiences. In fact, this is what really keeps me on my toes as a consultant because every environment is truly unique. Like astrology for architecture, feng shui explores how the influences of the earth and cosmos combine to produce energy fields that affect us in very mundane ways. A house type or its location can reveal the ease or difficulty the occupants will have in getting pregnant or the likelihood of whether or not the home will be burglarized. Both good and bad events and circumstances can be predicted when enough data is gathered. Just like a weatherman who gives the forecast, a feng shui practitioner can predict to what extent the occupants of a building will prosper or be undermined in a given environment.

Think of any structure as a living organism interacting with all its contents, as well as the immediate exterior environment. The relationship between feng shui and your home is much like the relationship you have with your family or your business partner. Some family members support each other, while others challenge each other and cause tension. The house or building is like another personality that you have to interact with.

How much can feng shui knowledge help people? The answer depends on what expectations a person has, as well as how completely they follow through with alterations to their environment. Basically, feng shui can help a lot. It can have seemingly miraculous results for some, while for others the results are more gradual or subtle. I consider myself a skeptic regarding many things, but after working with feng shui principles for so many years and with thousands of clients, I am no longer skeptical about these particular theories. I can confidently say, almost 100 percent of my clients agree with my diagnosis of their homes or businesses. I usually begin the consultation knowing almost nothing about the personal or professional lives of my clients, yet they overwhelmingly validate my assessments. Since I am in no way psychic, I can only assume feng shui is a physical reality.

Of all the things we have at our disposal in these modern times, feng shui is just one more feature to help us live to our potential. For instance, if you are trying to be healthy, not only will you want to eat nutritious food, but you will recognize how your physical surroundings affect your health. Some aspects are obvious, like not working around secondhand smoke, but the non-obvious environment can even include the colors and materials used in your furnishings.

The concept of inanimate objects affecting your health and well-being is new to Westerners. If it is not your destiny to be extremely rich, all the feng shui maneuvers for prosperity will not drastically change your financial status. However, most people are elated if their incomes improve by 20 to 50 percent concurrent with changes they have made.

A client of mine had a low-paying job when we first met. I could see his house had great potential to help him prosper. He followed through with about five recommendations, which included placing certain elements and objects around the house. He probably spent under $500 for those changes. A couple years later, he called to tell me his whole life changed shortly after applying those remedies. He bought a franchise in another city and turned it into the company's biggest producing location in the world. He also had plans to buy several more franchises around the country. It is my own humble opinion that good feng shui *and* destiny intersected to bring about his sudden change of fortune. He has, ever since, been gushing with appreciation and crediting feng shui for the dramatic turn of luck.

Feng shui is also very helpful in reducing an existing problem or preventing something bad from happening in the first place. Unfortunately, if you have been diagnosed with six months to live, feng shui alterations to your house will probably not save you. For the skeptic who feels all these maneuvers are placebos, I have these responses:

1. The assumption it's "all in one's mind" is actually an acknowledgment of an even more subtle metaphysical premise. It is admitting to believing you can, in fact, change your reality just with your

thoughts and willful projection. If that were possible I would be a tall, thin blonde. I wish, as a human race, we all were so evolved but I'm afraid it just ain't so. The real skeptic would call this "magical thinking."

2. It is also possible to think everything in life is a placebo, even the high blood pressure medicine your Western doctor has prescribed. This type of skepticism can be taken to an extreme, believing nothing and nobody really affects anything or anyone else. Of course, this is absurd.

So I will proceed, with the assumption my readers are capable of putting their hard-core skepticism aside, at least for the duration of this book. I guarantee you will learn some things that can improve your life and I thank you in advance for being open-minded.

THE MOST IMPORTANT AREAS OF YOUR HOUSE

The most important areas of your house to be concerned with include the following:

● *Your bedroom.* Most people spend six to eight hours per night—roughly $1/4$ to $1/3$ of your life—in this room. If the feng shui (i.e. energy) of this room is out of balance, it weighs heavily against the ranking of the entire house.

● *The entrance you most frequently use.* You pass through this area often so it makes sense for you to be influenced by it. It is also the mouth of the house, where outside energies are most easily carried inside.

● *Any other room or part of the house in which you spend at least an hour each day* could also be scrutinized by feng shui standards. If you have an income-generating home office, that room ranks fairly high in importance.

Often, readers who are new to feng shui will not know how to prioritize the most important areas of their homes or work areas. They treat each flaw with equal concern and fret about minor details, while the big picture eludes them. This book has just made it very clear what your priorities should be: where you sleep, where you enter, where you spend most of your waking hours.

This is not to say kitchens or bathrooms do not affect the occupants. They most certainly do, and examples will be given throughout this book about relevant aspects of every part of a house or building. No place is perfect, but with enough feng shui knowledge, it is possible to create a space that is nearly perfect for many decades.

Presently, there is a tremendous amount of misinformation perpetuated in popular feng shui books. They are like fad diet books. This misinformation exists for several reasons. First, there are many different schools of feng shui and each has its own priorities. When only one branch or aspect of feng shui is explored, it seriously limits having a holistic, comprehensive understanding of the big picture. I helped one of my clients, a dentist, find a house in the affluent area of Corona del Mar, California. His grandfather, in China, gave him a small checklist of things he should consider for a good feng shui house. The list was embarrassingly simplistic but it was difficult for me, the pale face, to convince this Chinese doctor I knew more about feng shui than his grandfather from the old country.

Another reason for the continuing proliferation of misinformation is because feng shui comes from a very superstitious culture, where folk remedies, rituals and spiritual beliefs from long ago have gotten mixed up with what I believe to be authentic, timeless and universal principles.

Feng shui is based on laws of physics, natural cycles, common sense and good design. Feng shui affects everyone, regardless of whether they are aware of it or not. Enduring folk remedies have, unfortunately, made feng shui appear relevant only to Chinese culture—a serious misunderstanding. As an example, the dragon is a mythical symbol from Chinese culture associated with good luck. In American culture, a rabbit's foot or a horseshoe carry similar connotations. However, just as a symbol, neither a dragon or a rabbit's foot, nor a horseshoe can energetically change the composition of a room or bring you extra good fortune. Sorting through all the feng shui myths and superstitions is an exhausting undertaking, but I will expose some of the more common and annoying ones.

A third reason for the misinformation is the fact that many New Age practitioners have tried to reinvent the wheel. New theories, new remedies and new ways to diagnose buildings have cropped up just since the 1970s and the unsuspecting public assumes these New Age interpretations are ancient, when actually they are not. Many of these notions have come from the overactive McMinds of people who have no business wielding such power over trusting clients. At the same time, I am not saying all things ancient are correct or worthy of preserving. We often put ancient, mysterious beliefs and practices on a pedestal and believe it is important, even sacred, to preserve them. A nostalgic attachment to a simpler past just doesn't do it for me. I, for one, do not believe everything worth learning was learned in kindergarten. As well, you won't read in these pages any literal references to "evil spirits." Toxic, unbalanced or negative, yes, but not evil.

The New Age version of feng shui includes a self-absorbed, consumer-driven fantasy of a "wealth corner." Like Santa Claus, there is no such thing as a wealth corner. Yet the public has heard so much about this imaginary part of the house, it has become difficult to correct such notions. It reminds me of the saying, "If you hear a lie enough times, it becomes a truth." In truth, there are several areas of a house with the potential to help increase one's income, and those areas will be revealed throughout this book. The word "potential" means *you* also have to participate in your own success—rarely does it just fall in one's lap.

Even people who appear to be luckier than others won't sustain such momentum for their entire lives. From a Taoist perspective, everything is cyclical. If you live in a rich city inside a rich country, you have more potential than a person living in a poor city inside a poor country. So, if you hang out in the most positive parts of your own house, you increase your potential to do better than if you spend time in the more negative areas.

People in the feng shui industry, as well as consumers, often do not like to hear anything critical about a certain school of feng shui or a select practitioner's consulting style. Since the whole concept of feng shui is based on a metaphysical outlook on life, many people find it hard to believe any feng shui advice could be harmful if it is dispensed with sincerity. Some people simply do not want to believe there are feng shui practitioners more concerned with making money than practicing the truth. Unfortunately, I am not exaggerating. I know of a so-called master who scares his clients with bad news, then tries to persuade them to buy his expensive original paintings as if they were remedies against their coming doom. Being Chinese, he looks the part but is obviously a disgrace to the whole industry.

Living in these volatile times, I have noticed some people don't have the nervous systems to withstand any controversy. They strive for feng shui–correctness much as one would political correctness, not wanting to step on anyone's toes. When I first started reading about feng shui myself, I found out about these discrepancies and contradictions and was annoyed and bewildered as to why they were so. Having studied and experienced feng shui on a deep level, I know I provide a great service correcting this misinformation and making my contribution toward abolishing the false feng shui schools. Incidentally, this is not a new problem. Even centuries ago, feng shui masters disputed between the false schools and the authentic ones.

It should be known that, historically, false schools and books were intentionally created to confuse people and prevent the real knowledge and power from leaking to the masses. Chinese emperors and the wealthy had access to feng shui masters and wanted to keep the knowledge to themselves.

As you read through this book you will find inherent method and precision in many of the theories. Feng shui is not supposed to be based on a thinking-makes-it-so mentality. One popular New Age school of feng shui teaches its students "intention is 90 percent of the cure." This whole notion contradicts the practices of feng shui because, if thinking made it so, wouldn't we all just trash the theories and become masters of meditation? In case you feel being critical of certain feng shui schools is mean-spirited and inconsistent with the Taoist philosophy of nonjudgment, please know the information and opinions I express are for the ultimate good of all, even if I have to ruffle some feathers along the way. There are rules, calculations, ultimate rights and wrongs—just as two plus two equals four—even if someone wants you to believe it equals five.

THE FOUR MAJOR COMPONENTS OF AN EVALUATION

In order to not be superstitious, you can correctly assume a feng shui evaluation involves many variables and each property is truly unique. There are four major components in a feng shui audit:

1. *Time.* Even after a decade of explosive interest in feng shui in the Western world, few people have heard the critical importance of *when* a structure is built. Feng shui used to be called "Time and Space School" because the age of a building reveals so many of its unseen influences. Aside from the semi-permanent energy created at the time of construction, new energies can also enter a building when it is significantly remodeled. Also, changing yearly cycles (like having a guest in your home) will influence or trigger the permanent energies. For example, if your home is inherently prone to having a fire, it will most likely happen in the year and month when there are added irritants to its vulnerable location. To quote a fellow colleague, "If feng shui were a vegetable, it would be an onion." This is to say, there are so many layers. Chapters Four and Five go into greater detail about the aspect of time and the various house types from certain construction periods.

2. *Orientation.* The direction a building faces, using precise compass measurements, will also reveal a tremendous amount of insight into the personality of a building and how it affects the occupants. So much of advanced feng shui is relevant to compass directions, only a fool would call himself a feng shui master who doesn't incorporate compass calculations into his or her analysis. Throughout this book you will learn about how each direction can affect family members, relationships and health issues.

3. *Environment.* Included in Form School feng shui is the study of how the total environment interacts with people—and animals (yes, animals are also affected by feng shui). As an example, if the energy in your bedroom indicates back pain and your pet sleeps there with you, it is possible for your pet to also experience back pain. Environment includes the interior as well as the exterior, and both natural and man-made features. There is a difference in

having a hill behind your house or having a small pond or swimming pool. There is a difference between a metal sculpture situated in front of a building versus a large tree. Everything, living or supposedly dead, dormant or inanimate can have an effect on a person. If you don't initially believe this, just consider how most of us are controlled by food.

4. *People.* The more subjective part of feng shui includes the personal component. What may be a healthy and invigorating environment for one individual could be overly stimulating for a different type of person. Variables include a person's age, gender, lifestyle habits, occupation, marital status and personality. There are house types good for single people who want exciting love lives. However, the same house could be quite detrimental to a married couple. A building that attracts legal conflict could be ruinous for the average person, but a bonus for a law firm.

A comprehensive feng shui evaluation should examine the blending of influences in the four major categories of time, orientation, environment and people. Not considering all of these categories of influence reduces feng shui to generic at best. At its worst, feng shui has been ridiculed as being nothing more than an exercise in pseudo-spiritual interior decorating. Real feng shui is as real as gravity.

The New Age spin-off versions come replete with exotic names, such as the Black Hat Tantric Sect School or the Pyramid School. Some of the New Age adaptations contain beliefs and practices that are actually complementary to what I call real feng shui, but some of these adaptations are in direct conflict with or contradiction to what I know to be true. Examples and comparisons will be highlighted throughout this book so you can come to your own conclusions.

DIFFERENT SCHOOLS OF FENG SHUI

According to feng shui scholar Master Joseph Yu, there are technically more than 100 different schools or traditions. Some are almost identical to each other, some quite different. Historically, some schools were more popular than others for certain periods of time. I can only assume when there were less durable living structures or people spent more time outdoors (farming or dealing directly with the forces of nature) exterior landscapes were studied more intensely than they are presently, as we mostly live and work inside buildings.

FORM SCHOOL FENG SHUI

Form School feng shui studies the landscape and how natural features, such as mountains and river courses, can affect the health and well-being of those living nearby. In modern times, tall buildings can exert influences similar to mountains. Streets and highways can behave as virtual rivers. Weather or climate conditions and seasonal changes will influence how large groups of people feel. Form School feng shui can also be taken indoors. If a gust of wind can forcefully push through a mountain range, a less detectable flow of air currents can also push through a hallway. Form School also interprets the shapes of all things, from a house's floor plan down to the dimensions of a piece of furniture.

Form School observes how chi (air currents) flows, causing either beneficial encouragement of healthful energies or an unwelcome barrage of negative influences. Like all feng shui traditions, Form School is about balance. The air currents are considered most healthful when they flow neither too quickly nor too slowly, like a gently flowing breeze. This gives way to an aspect of Chinese Metaphysics, which pervades all schools of feng shui, and it is called Yin-Yang Theory.

YIN-YANG THEORY

Yin-Yang theory is the study of opposites and extremes. The Yin aspect relates to characteristics that are dark, still, dormant, small, constrictive, closed in, cold and damp. The Yang aspect is evident in environments that are light, lively, moving, big, expansive, open, warm and dry. Any aspect of yin or yang that is too extreme or prolonged will throw the space out of balance and cause problems. Living in a chronically dark and damp space will make almost anyone sickly and depressed, but living in a space that is always bright and dry can make occupants irritable as well. The goal of feng shui is to strike a balance appropriate for the function of the room and who is using it. This is one area where interior designers have either an instinctual or a trained approach to balancing an environment.

FIVE ELEMENT THEORY

Another branch of traditional feng shui is called Five Element Theory, which considers the elements of water, wood, fire, earth and metal. The five natural elements can be powerful remedies, symbolically as well as literally. Einstein said, "Space is not just empty space, but a tightly woven fabric of time and space." His comment implies that an empty room is teeming with energy and molecular interactions. The contents of the room will then intermingle with the chi of the room and cause a kind of interaction. This reaction will affect occupants in a predictable way. Here is a quick exercise: Close your eyes and imagine sitting in a square room with sky blue walls. Then switch to imagining yourself in a triangular room painted red. You probably had an immediate reaction. Feng shui is usually more unconscious, but powerful and enduring nonetheless.

Water

Water is one of the five basic elements—the "shui" of feng shui. When you need the water element to correct an imbalance somewhere in your house, real water must be used, not a picture of water. Clean, circulating water is more effective than still water. This is why fountains and aquariums are widely recommended by just about every school of feng shui. They are practical ways of getting water into areas that would not normally have any. The colors blue and black, on a large scale, are considered a vibratory representation of real water. So, if you painted an entire room blue, it would resonate some of the water element.

Wood

Wood is an element that is somewhat misunderstood. Wood furniture is mostly dormant, so there is no harm in having wood furniture just about anywhere, including wood floors. When you want to use wood as a remedying element, a live green plant is effective. A large display of green color, such as wall paint or carpet, can also work.

Fire

Fire is an extreme element and placing it anywhere can be very good or very bad. Most Westerners who have not studied feng shui deeply do not know how to use the fire element correctly. In Chinese culture, the color red symbolizes happiness, fertility and prosperity. In America, it is a color associated with passion, power, sexuality and appetite. Above and beyond any cultural or psychological associations with red, large displays of it vibrate heat, the fire element. Painting a door red for luck or power is a popular feng shui myth that is used incorrectly most of the time. In my experience, fire colors used in the wrong locations can trigger accidents, miscarriages, divorces and a whole list of undesirable events. The fire element can be anything of significant size that is red, maroon, burgundy, hot pink or cranberry in color.

Earth

The earth element is represented by anything made from soil or stone. Objects of clay, ceramic, brick, concrete and marble possess the vibration of earth. Natural healing crystals like rose quartz and amethyst are also earth elements. Anything largely yellow, orange or brown in color represents the earth element. I don't believe man-made crystals possess much healing value, although they are popularly used in some of the New Age spin-off schools.

Metal

Anything made out of copper, brass, bronze, pewter, steel, silver or gold is a metal element. Metallic colors such as white and gray also enhance an environment in need of metal but real metal is best. Much of our furnishings and decor can be metal and can be inconspicuously incorporated into a living space or work area. A row of metal file cabinets would definitely qualify as a metal remedy. In other words, it is not necessary to purchase exotic metal Chinese knickknacks. A set of golf clubs in the appropriate location can do as much good as a strand of Chinese gold coins or brass Mandarin ducks. I like to see people use heavy pieces of raw, inexpensive copper or brass and not be timid with their metal remedies. Twenty-five to 30 pounds of metal are usually the minimum weight needed to affect a 10 foot by 10 foot room. Larger rooms usually need larger remedies. In later chapters you will be instructed on some good areas to place these elements.

The five elements have three distinct relationships with each other. They should not all be represented in each room because they would actually cancel each other out. The myth that states all the elements together create balance is not true. In other words, you should not attempt to decorate every room with equal doses of the five elements to create balance. Commercialized attempts at this can be seen in copper fountains that have stones in the bowl with candles and plants incorporated in the container (water, wood, fire, earth, and metal). One popular author recommends placing all the elements in one location as a last resort when things are going wrong in your life. She refers to this as her "cover your butt cure." This makes as much sense as swallowing everything in your medicine cabinet when you don't know why you are ill.

As an example, water nurtures wood and strengthens it. It is part of the productive cycle of the elements. Also, wood feeds or strengthens fire within the productive cycle, but water extinguishes fire. It controls it and can destroy it. So, usually water and fire are not put together. There are some rare instances when exceptions are made for advanced reasons.

In Figure 1-1, the productive cycle shows the natural, willing flow of the five elements. Figure 1-2, the destructive (or dominating) cycle, shows the power one element can have over another, even to the point of destroying it.

Some of the elements do not have to be seen in order for them to work, such as metal. You could have 100 pounds of iron weights

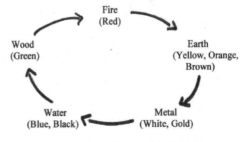

Figure 1-1. Productive Cycle
of the Five Elements

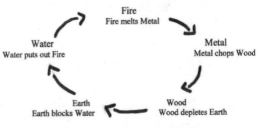

Figure 1-2. Domination Cycle
of the Five Elements

tucked away behind something or under a piece of furniture, which would work as well as a bronze statue out on display. Conversely, fire (red color) must be very noticeable in a room or it is not adequate. In other words, a red book on a shelf is not enough of the fire element, but a red rug can cover enough surface area to have an effect on the room's magnetic field.

When a room has a destructive combination of elements (in the unseen energies), such as metal destroying wood, the third cycle of the elements is introduced to correct the problem. You are not expected to know at this point how to determine if there is a destructive cycle of elements going on in any given room. In later chapters you will be given existing examples to refer to.

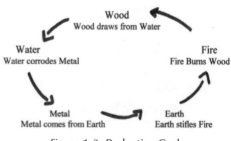

Figure 1-3. Reductive Cycle of the Five Elements

The third cycle is called the reductive cycle, which is essentially using a corrective element to mitigate a problem between two others (see Figure 1-3). If metal is destroying wood, water can be introduced to strengthen wood. If wood is destroying earth (the way a plant can deplete soil), fire is added to strengthen the earth.

The reductive element acts to mitigate and transmute the conflict within the destructive cycle. The reductive element is like a peacemaker breaking up a fight or taking away the power from a bully and handing it over to the underdog. Specific examples will be given of how to correct problematic areas when case study house types are described in future chapters.

These productive and destructive element relationships are not visible or obvious when entering a room, but they can be revealed through time and direction calculations, and stimulated by very physical objects in the room. These same energies may even become activated by the very shape of the room. As an example, a normal square room can help keep some unseen influences in check, but a really awkward or chaotic arrangement will only make things worse.

The Flying Star School (Shyun Kung School)—a highly accurate way to diagnose a building—is sometimes referred to as one of the classical schools among Westerners. This form of feng shui incorporates calculations based on when a structure has been built in combination with its compass orientation. I have been practicing the Flying Star School since 1992 and can vouch for its accuracy. It allows practitioners to use the five elements in the most sophisticated ways. It is crucial to know not only where the best and worst areas of a building are, but when their influence will be most active. No other school of feng shui besides the Flying Star School addresses the aspect of timing. It explains perfectly why people and businesses flourish for a certain period of time, then meet misfortune later while still inhabiting the same building.

The East-West School of feng shui is sometimes called the Eight Mansions or Pa Chai School. Some aspects of this school are quite useful, such as determining a person's best sleeping direction. Other aspects of the East-West School are very generic to only eight basic house types and not as conclusive as the Flying Star School. In Chapter Six, I will highlight some of the more practical uses of the East-West School.

In the Western world, the most popular school of feng shui in the 1990s was the Black Hat Tantric Buddhist Sect. This group now often calls their school simply BTB. I guess this is like Kentucky Fried Chicken going by KFC. While it is still the most popularly known school in the Western world (with the most prolific authors), it is the least authentic and reliable of all the schools. This is not to say Black Hat practitioners do not attain good results. Many of them achieve positive results, in spite of their not always understanding why. Unfortunately, there are many stories of wrong remedies backfiring and making things worse. As outlined, there are five essential elements; so even someone who doesn't understand Five Element Theory still has a 20 percent chance of using the right element by accident.

The Black Hat School came into being in the 1970s and this is the only school of feng shui many Westerners were aware of until decades later, when more qualified traditional practitioners began to speak up, teach, consult and write their own books and articles. Black Hat practitioners have been misled by its founder and initial disciples into believing their version of feng shui stems from a lineage with Black Hat Tantric Buddhism. According to some historic research, Buddha discouraged his disciples from practicing feng shui because, like all the other predictive arts, feng shui was seen as a distraction from meditation and part of the illusion. I personally went to a Buddhist temple with Master Sang as one of our case study classes. We were instructed to be very low-key when walking around the temple and to not flash our compasses. It was explained that an obvious feng shui audit would be offensive to the members of the temple.

The creator of the Black Hat School is a man who was originally known as Professor Thomas Lin Yun. Over the years, his devoted following renamed him Master Lin Yun and elevated him to "Grand" Master. While it is debatable whether or not he is a feng shui master in the old-world sense, he most certainly is a marketing genius in the twentieth century sense.

In fairness to the Black Hat School, most of their practitioners do incorporate many universally understood Form School theories. For instance, every feng shui school will teach that a front door directly aligned with a back door is a bad arrangement. This is because the chi or air currents will move too swiftly from point A to point B. The potential result is that occupants with this type of floor plan will find it

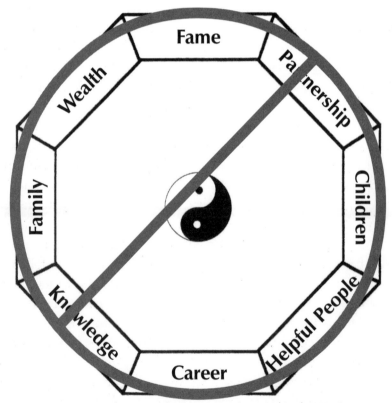

Figure 1-4. The New Age Ba-gua was invented in the 1970s and is not considered authentic feng shui.

hard to save money. Strange, but true. Every school of feng shui will track the negative and positives forces of yin-yang theory (opposites and extremes).

But it is the Black Hat School that created the New Age Ba-gua, sometimes referred to as McFeng shui by its most vocal critics. It is a "one size fits all" notion claiming that certain areas of your house correlate with specific life stations such as wealth, marriage and career (see Figure 1-4). This is not ancient feng shui, rather the board game version. It works for several reasons, including the fact that a good percentage of the population is easily influenced and will respond to the dreaded placebo effect. In fact, the Black Hat practitioners constantly instill their clients with intention practices. If it isn't authentic feng shui, you could consider it on a par with goal setting, coaching or hypnosis.

Another phenomenon in the West is the majority of interest in feng shui coming from women. Many men reject or make fun of the idea, even calling it "fake shui." This has always been ironic to me since historically it was a man's profession. Women could not study it openly. Feng shui derives some of its wisdom from such male-dominated fields as astronomy, geology, topography, probability theory, time-space theory and architecture. There are stories from feng shui history about women trying to steal the information and not being allowed to practice it openly.

Some of my most successful clients are men who take feng shui very seriously and say they believe it has given them a winning edge over their professional competitors. Some of them were quite skeptical in the beginning, but ultimately male clients tend to have better follow-through than female. Male intelligence dictates if you pay for advice, comply with the recommendations to either prove or disprove it. More often, it is women who procrastinate or make excuses for not following through. While the average man on the street worries his feng shui–indoctrinated wife or girlfriend is participating in a snake oil marketing scam, some mathematicians and physicists relate to feng shui theory with less skepticism. In my own client relationships, I find doctors, engineers and physicists—the scientific minds—more validating than the celebrities. At the same time, I owe a lot to my entertainment industry clients, for their open minds especially.

Whatever school of feng shui you are exposed to or relate to better, just know you can't argue with results. If a certain remedy works for you and your life has improved because of it, that is what all sincere practitioners are striving for on behalf of their clients. If your life has not improved after following someone's recommendations, let them know about it so they can investigate the situation, refine their methods and work toward improving their knowledge for you and future clients.

CHAPTER TWO

SHAPES OF THINGS TO COME

Everything physical has a shape and dimension—and size matters. A shape that is harmful on a large scale may not be a problem on a small scale. For example, a corner edge of a piece of furniture is sometimes referred to as a poison arrow. If this corner is angled toward you all day, there may be the possibility of feeling uncomfortable. This case is not as severe as a large building with its corner angled toward a smaller building. In order to understand shape better, it is important to first discuss the concept of chi (pronounced "chee" and sometimes written as qi).

Chi is energy. Chi is matter. Sometimes called "life force energy," chi is in the air currents moving around in a room almost undetectably, or in the exact opposite way, such as heavy winds that can knock down trees. The chi between two closely situated buildings will create a wind tunnel. Chi can build up speed moving down a long corridor and have a negative effect at the end of its course.

There are two basic types of chi. Shen-chi refers to energies that are benign and health-inducing. Shen-chi supports harmony and balance in an environment. This may be like a person's body having good or bad circulation; it can affect so many areas. Even a kind, likable person could be described as possessing good chi or shen-chi.

21

Sha-chi describes an environment or circumstance where the physical space becomes harmful, unhealthful, irritated or accident-prone. Also, a person with a lot of anger inside will project sha-chi onto himself and others. Sometimes a chronically negative person can be sensed the moment she walks into a room.

Examples of shen-chi and sha-chi can be seen or felt everywhere in the most mundane ways. If you simply feel wonderful in a particular setting, the space may likely possess shen-chi. By comparison, if you go somewhere that makes you feel uncomfortable and you can't wait to leave, that is a strong indication of sha-chi.

Below are some more examples of shen-chi and sha-chi:

SHEN-CHI

● A room where the ventilation is good
● A room where the lighting is good
● A room that is clean and tidy
● A room with pleasant views from the windows or balconies
● A normal floor plan that does not have any awkwardly shaped rooms

SHA-CHI

● A space that smells bad, like mildew or something rotting
● A space that is dirty or feels oppressive
● A place that has threatening or depressing things in view, such as sharp items or broken items
● Cracks in the flooring or foundation

These points are totally obvious, which is why people in other professions erroneously assume feng shui is just a spiritual twist to what they already do. Of course, there is so much more to identifying shen-chi or sha-chi. The above lists constitute only the raw basics.

HOW DIFFERENT SHAPES OF HOUSES AFFECT YOU

Shapes have a different impact depending on whether they occur on a small or large scale. As an example, a round table invites more group participation. It helps create a social environment where people feel equal among each other. Round tables at restaurants can encourage people to eat more and faster. In a round building (e.g., Capitol Records in Hollywood) the swirling energy may be too intense for some. A round building can easily be a place where people have a hard time focusing and even feel gossipy or argumentative. This is why we can't always say a shape is inherently good or bad feng shui. It has to be a comparative study.

There needs to be an understanding of the size of the shape, what other shapes are surrounding it, how the space is used, and who is using it. Artistic people tend to do better in odd-shaped rooms or buildings than less creative types. An important feature in determining if a shape is balanced or not is the adjacent environment. As an example, a room that is very angular with sharp, hard architectural lines might be balanced out with more curving, rounded furnishings. This is an application of yin-yang theory.

SQUARE

The square is considered a balanced shape and is associated with the earth element. Since earth is connected with businesses that deal with the literal earth, it is believed a square building enhances commercial property associated with real estate, architecture, landscaping, design, city planning and warehouses or public storage. Square houses are not missing

Figure 2-1. The square.

any of their directional quadrants, a benefit that will become more obvious in a later chapter.

RECTANGLE

The rectangle is a variation on the square and is also considered balanced. However, if a rectangular building is extremely narrow, the occupants can feel the pressure and constriction. As an example, a

Figure 2-2. The rectangle.

house (usually a duplex) or a storefront that is six times as long as it is wide will not feel comfortable (see Figure 2-3).

Figure 2-3. The severe rectangle.

TRIANGLE

Fortunately, there are hardly any triangular houses. This shape can make people argumentative, accident-prone and generally aggressive. Rooms in this shape are sometimes carved out of insufficient space to make a square room. I have been in office spaces and treatment rooms shaped like triangles and have found it doesn't take long to feel uncomfortable in them.

The triangle shape is associated with fire, like a flame that peaks at the top. Buildings that are tall and come to a point at the top (like a church steeple) are grouped into the fire-

Figure 2-4. The triangle.

type building category. This does not mean they are literally prone to catching on fire. Instead, it has more to do with the shape of other buildings surrounding them and their relationship. In the cycle of the elements, fire strengthens earth. If you had a fire-shaped building on a street along with earth-shaped buildings, in a subtle way you could say the fire-shaped building is strengthening the earth-shaped structures around it. The relationship is complementary. If feng shui were used in city planning, this would be a consideration.

OBLONG

An oblong shape is generally harmless because it has no pointy edges. Oblong furnishings could be placed just about anywhere. An oblong pool or a kidney-shaped pool

Figure 2-5. The oblong or oval.

is preferable to a rectangular pool.

COLUMN

Like a tall tree, the column shape is associated with the wood element. This shape should not be a problem unless its height is extreme.

PYRAMID

For ages people have given mystical connotations to pyramids, as with Egyptian tombs, but they are not appropriate shapes for the living. The upper part becomes sharp, a triangle, and energy will not flow harmoniously for people trying

Figure 2-6. The column.

to live or work inside. I have had firsthand experience staying at the Luxor Hotel in Las Vegas, where I was very uncomfortable for three days. To exacerbate the pyramid shape of the Hotel, the rooms themselves are also very angular and odd-shaped. I do not believe I was imagining my irritation or discomfort.

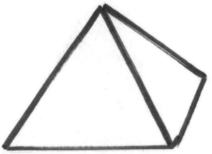

Figure 2-7. The pyramid.

HEXAGON OR OCTAGON

Like the pyramid, hexagonal or octagonal shapes are associated with some kind of sacred geometry, but they are not comfortable shapes to dwell in. This does not mean your octagonal dining table has bad feng shui; it is only a problem on a large scale, such as with buildings.

Figure 2-8. The hexagram.

Figure 2-9. The octagon.

U-SHAPED

The severe U-shaped house can either have its empty space toward the street or toward the back of the property. Each means something different in relation to how the occupants are affected. When the missing area is on the front side, it is like a person with no face. The

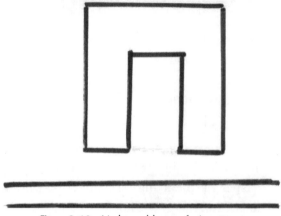

Figure 2-10. U-shaped house facing street.

people who live in this shape house may be very private, not showing their face or personalities easily. When the missing space is in the back, it is like a person who has no spine or a chair with no backing (see

Figure 2-11). There is no structural support for the occupants. They are all face. People in this type of house may be well known or extroverted, but they don't have the backing to support them financially. An extreme example might be a famous person who ultimately goes bankrupt.

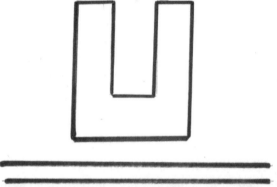

Figure 2-11. U-shaped house facing away from street.

L-SHAPED

The L-shaped house should not be confused with a square or rectangular house that simply has an extension to its square shape. Figure 2-13 shows a rectangular shape with an extension. This is common with house types that have attached garages or later addi-

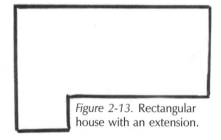

Figure 2-13. Rectangular house with an extension.

tions, but is not considered an L-shaped house.

Figure 2-12.
L-shaped house.

The L-shape should really look like two rectangles joined together, to be considered an L-shaped house. The elbow, or point where they are joined together contains the most stress energetically. Referring back to Figure 2-12, the kitchen is right in the elbow of the shape. This is not as bad as having a master bedroom there. The L-shaped house is not necessarily a bad house if it has other redeeming features. It is usually looked at as two houses connected (see Figures 2-14 and 2-15). In order to know which section is part of the longer rectangle, you need to understand how the groupings of rooms will determine this. The L-shaped house in Figure 2-12 would be divided up in two parts like Figure 2-14. The grouping of the kitchen, dining room and living room constitute the more yang or lively part of the house, while the bedrooms and bathroom constitute the more yin side of the house.

In every mechanical rule or guideline in feng shui theory, there should also be a space reserved for subjective interpretation. Some people simply do not like certain shapes and this does not mean it is automatically negative or harmful. As an example, even if you hate the taste of tofu, eating it will not hurt you.

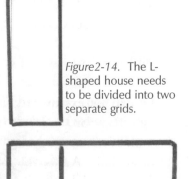

Figure 2-14. The L-shaped house needs to be divided into two separate grids.

Figure 2-15. Alternate way to divide L-shaped house.

The shape of a land parcel will also affect the house placed on that location:

● A triangular lot will contribute to accidents and arguments (see Figure 2-16).

● An odd-shaped lot can cause an uneven flow of chi surrounding the property.

● Odd lot shapes can often be squared out through landscaping features, such as fences, walls or hedges (see Figure 2-17).

● Lot shapes that narrow severely toward the back squeeze or constrict the chi. This can also make it hard for the occupants to save their money.

Figure 2-16. House on a triangular lot that narrows in the back.

LIGHTNING BOLT HOUSE

The house in Figure 2-18 has a floor plan resembling the zigzag formation of a lightning bolt. This is a high-drama house. Occupants can become very lucky when they first move in, but after a while misfortune strikes. The erratic flow of air currents inside causes a vacillation between good and bad luck. The best

Figure 2-17. A triangular lot squared out with a fence.

correction for this house type is structural. Adding a room or enlarging a room can make the lightning bolt shape not so severe.

Figure 2-18.
Lightning bolt house.

Concerning lots, it is important to mention:

● When choosing land without any structures, there are a number of things to consider about the quality of the soil itself and its ability to store good chi. Land that does not possess good chi will be difficult to grow anything on. I once had a client who discovered after she moved in, that the contractor had buried in her backyard all the concrete and garbage from the previous teardown. It was impossible for her to plant trees.

● With knowledge of when a structure is to be built and the limits of its future orientation, some lots will naturally be better than others.

● When houses are situated too close to each other, sufficient light and privacy can be undermined. With the trend of building mansions on small lots these days, people in multi-million-dollar homes are still subjected to their neighbor's intimate household sounds.

● When a land parcel is basically square or rectangular but is missing a directional quadrant, the direction missing will indicate a potential deficiency in the lives or health of the occupants (see Figure 2-19). This will be covered more in the next chapter, but an example would be possible difficulty for occupants to conceive a boy if the east quadrant (associated with the eldest son in the family structure) was missing from their land.

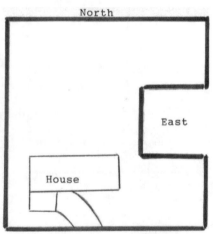

Figure 2-19. Square or rectangular lot missing an east quadrant.

SHARP CORNERS

In Form School feng shui, the shape (or form) of every landscape, building, interior floor plan, furnishing and object can be categorized for its potential meaning or effect on human beings. The shapes of mountains can be classified as readily as buildings. Shapes and images people commonly think of as threatening or dangerous, like sharp edges or constricted space, are viewed similarly in feng shui theory. The sharp

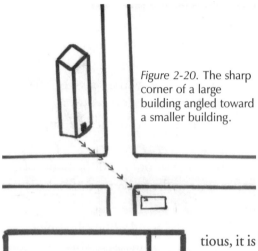

Figure 2-20. The sharp corner of a large building angled toward a smaller building.

Figure 2-21. Desk and back of chair aligned with room's interior column.

corner of a large building, angled toward a smaller building can send a strong line of sha-chi toward the smaller structure (see Figure 2-20). Again, this is sometimes called "poison arrows" in the arcane terminology. This direct line of energy could contribute to business struggles for the smaller space.

Although it sounds superstitious, it is based on how air currents move in a predictable way. In Figure 2-21, the corner of an interior column in an office, pointed at the occupant's back all day long could result in back pain.

On a more subtle level, we all know when we are on the receiving end of a "look that can kill," and sense the aggressive energy behind it. Most people feel uncomfortable if they are seated in a public place with their back to the main activities of the room. Most of us will also quickly change lanes on the freeway if a large truck moves in front of us, blocking our view.

What the feng shui masters from long ago used to refer to as "evil spirits" may today be recognized simply as a negative or threatening environment. Primitive and superstitious expressions still exist today in feng shui terminology and this tarnishes the more logical and accepted aspects of the practice. Chi will move in a particular way, based on the shape and size of a room. The location of doors and windows will vary its path. This is not dramatically different from tracking any type of movement for its immediate and residual effect. I don't know if a butterfly flapping its wings on another continent really impacts me or not, but we all know a traffic accident can have a residual effect on the time and activities of people 50 miles away.

EXAMPLES OF FLAWED FLOOR PLANS

A classic feng shui design flaw is a front door directly aligned with a back door. The concept is that the direct alignment of an entrance and exit will allow the chi to escape the house too quickly. This is like water spilling over its container. The end result of this design flaw is occupants who cannot save their money. A house that cannot properly store and circulate its chi cannot support the health and well-being of its occupants (see Figure 2-22). When a front door is aligned with a back door or a window, it may be easy to correct this problem with a partition screen, a live plant, lighting fixtures or any number of physical objects placed in between the two points. The goal is to slow down the direct path of chi. A necessary precaution is to make sure the object used to slow down the chi is not too bulky. This could slow down the energy too much and become a worse problem.

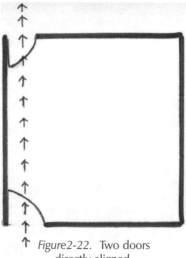

Figure 2-22. Two doors directly aligned.

Some of the biggest homebuilders in the country have modified their floor plans to accommodate the most basic feng shui design principles. Although they claim they do this for marketing reasons, it is truly because there is an ever-increasing demand for it. In one city in Southern California, 45 percent of the home buyers in 2002 were Asian.

Now that many people are aware of sharp edges and corners being considered bad feng shui, it should also be noted that the small corners of pieces of furniture are hardly a problem. Popular books have made readers panic unnecessarily when they state every bookshelf and nightstand is sending out harmful lines of sha-chi. There is no reason to be phobic about such tiny edges. The point where you need to be concerned is when there are large interior columns inside a room or, as mentioned before when buildings are angled toward each other, as in Figure 2-20.

The shape of furniture is hardly ever a problem. An exception might be when:

● The furniture is too large for the room, so by default people sit or sleep too close to odd-shaped piece or feel claustrophobic.

● Most of the time, the color and material substance of the furniture will have a bigger impact than its shape. Example, a wood bed frame will emanate a different energy than a metal bed frame.

● Some furniture is clearly uncomfortable or impractical.

The following illustrations show more examples of flawed floor plans:

● An entrance with a direct kitchen view (Figure 2-23) stirs the Pavlovian response to eat when not hungry.

● An entrance with a direct view to a bathroom (Figure 2-24) puts pressure on the bladder.

● An entrance looking directly down a long hallway with a bedroom door at the end, as in Figure 2-25, is seen as being too vulnerable—like being at the end of a wind tunnel.

● A congested entrance with a wall blocking the view to the living room acts as a clogged artery (see Figure 2-26).

● An entrance with too many options of where to go, as in Figure 2-27, causes confusion and irritation.

● A house with a bathroom in the center (Figure 2-28) stirs up too much energy.

● A house with the kitchen in the center could be prone to a literal fire (see Figure 2-29).

● A house with stairs aligned with the front door (Figure 2-30) leaks energy and money.

● Split-level stairs aligned with the front door create confusion and irritation (see Figure 2-31).

● A bedroom with the bed between the door and window, as in Figure 2-32, causes unrestful sleep.

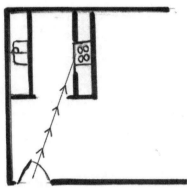

Figure 2-23. Entrance aligned directly with kitchen and view of stove.

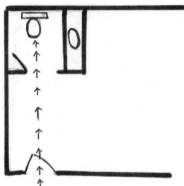

Figure 2-24. Entrance aligned directly with bathroom or toilet.

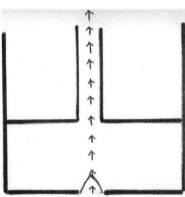

Figure 2-25. Entrance aligned directly with a long or narrow hallway.

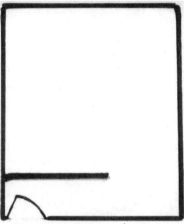

Figure 2-26. Congested entrance with blocked view caused by wall too close to door.

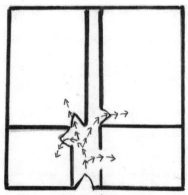

Figure 2-27. Confusing entrance with too may options.

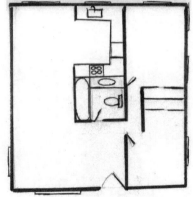

Figure 2-28. Heavily used bathroom in the center of the house.

Figure 2-29. Kitchen in the
center of the house.

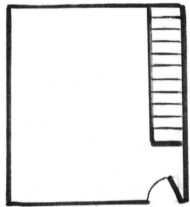

Figure 2-30. Stairs aligned directly
with an entrance.

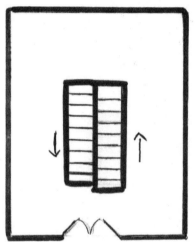

Figure 2-31. Stairs split up and down
aligned directly with an entrance.

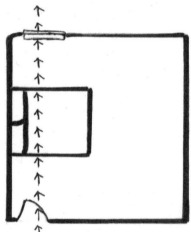

Figure 2-32. Bed aligned directly
between a door and a window.

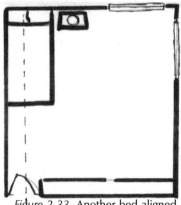

Figure 2-33. Another bed aligned
directly with a door.

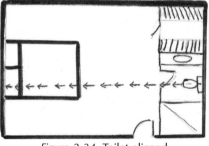

Figure 2-34. Toilet aligned
directly with bed.

www.kartardiamond.com

- If the bed is aligned directly with a door it will cause unrestful sleep (see Figure 2-33).

- A toilet aligned directly with a bed (Figure 2-34) creates the potential for health problems.

- Having several doors on the front side of the house is disorienting and will leak energy and money (see Figure 2-35).

- Beamed ceilings in a bedroom create downward pressure, which can cause marriage woes (see Figure 2-36).

- Sloped ceilings in a bedroom (Figure 2-37) create a chaotic flow causing unrestful sleep.

- A bed with no other placement option except under a low window is vulnerable to draft (see Figure 2-38).

Figure 2-35. Several entrance doors on the same wall.

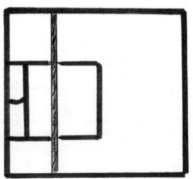

Figure 2-36. Exposed beam over bed.

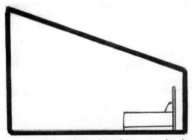

Figure 2-37. Sloped ceiling over bed, especially when bed is near lower part of ceiling.

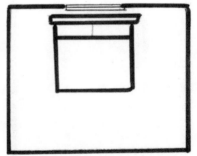

Figure 2-38. Bed against same wall as low window.

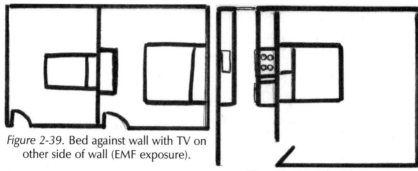

Figure 2-39. Bed against wall with TV on other side of wall (EMF exposure).

Figure 2-40. Bed against wall with a refrigerator or stove on other side of wall.

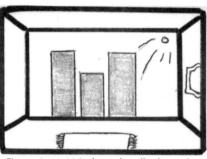

Figure 2-41. Windowed wall where the window goes from ceiling to floor.

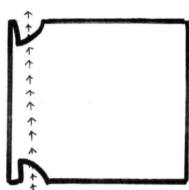

Figure 2-42. Two doors aligned directly opposite each other.

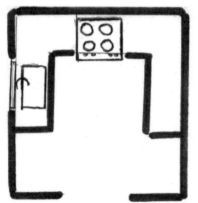

Figure 2-43. Stove forces cook to stand with back to kitchen entrance.

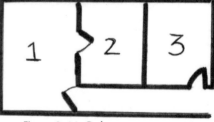

Figure 2-44. Only access to room 2 is through room 1.

● The electromagnetic field (EMF) exposure from a built-in TV wall unit sharing a wall with a bed, as in Figure 2-39, creates the potential for nervous system problems.

● A refrigerator against a wall with a bed on the other side is prone to the same EMF exposure (see Figure 2-40).

● Floor to ceiling windows with no borders (Figure 2-41) leak chi from the room.

● Doors aligned directly with each other across a hallway have the potential to leak energy (see Figure 2-42).

● A stove positioned so that the cook has her back to the room can make her accident-prone (Figure 2-43). However, more of an issue is made out of this than is necessary.

● Awkward additions, such as having to enter one room to get to another room as opposed to a central hallway, could jeopardize sufficient circulation of chi to the attached room (see Figure 2-44).

With the above examples, it should be obvious some problems are structural and some can be corrected with simple shifts in furniture or the addition of another item to slow down or manipulate a line of energy.

CHAPTER THREE

IS THAT A COMPASS IN YOUR POCKET

(or Are You Just Glad to See Me)?

No matter what the New Age version of feng shui has to say or add to this ancient Chinese practice, historically the compass has been the essential tool of the trade. And it is still relevant in modern times. Everything is relative to directions; without knowing how to use the compass, a feng shui analysis will be severely limited and general at best. Even Form School feng shui must incorporate the knowledge of what directions can mean. For example, a beautiful waterfall to the east of your house will have a different effect than a beautiful waterfall to the west of your house. An ugly view to your northeast will have a different effect than the same ugly view if it is to the southwest.

Feng shui is not supposed to be an intuitive free-for-all where someone can dismiss the defined energy that comes from each direction. Direction is at the root of all classical feng shui applications, even Yin-House feng shui, which concerns itself with the selection of a proper gravesite. It was believed where Grandpa Chang was buried could have an influence on up to three generations of descendants.

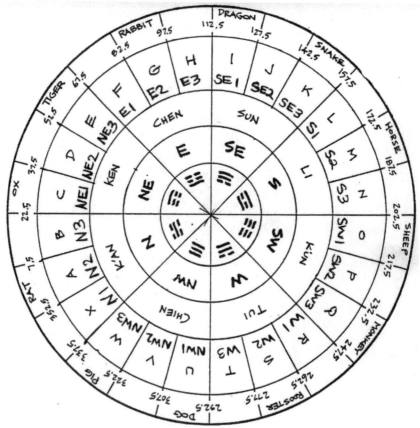

Figure 3-1. The compass.

Figure 3-1 shows the 15-degree increments of the compass and the important cut-off points you will need to pay attention to when you do your own compass reading.

PERFORMING AN ACCURATE COMPASS READING

1. Get a good quality compass that delineates all 360 degrees.

2. Stand outside the property and hold your compass level and parallel to the front exterior wall.

3. Stand 10–20 feet away from the property.

4. Do not do your compass reading inside a building—the metal infrastructure could make the reading inaccurate.

A Western compass will automatically point to magnetic north (0 degrees). A Chinese compass will automatically point to magnetic south (180 degrees). Once you see where north or south is located, you will be able to see what direction your house faces in relation to it (see

Figure 3-2). In Figure 3-2, if a person is holding a compass in front of a house and the compass points to north (at the angle shown), the house faces southeast in relation to where north really is.

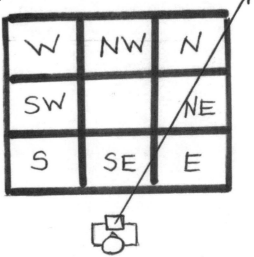

Make sure you are not standing near any metal objects, such as a car or metal gate because it will throw your compass off.

If you are trying to do a reading on a large commercial building with a lot of

Figure 3-2. If a house faces southeast, the compass will point north toward the back right-hand corner of the house.

metal infrastructure, you may have to stand across the street to get away from it disrupting your compass. If there is another large building across the street, you may have to find a residential street nearby that you are sure is parallel to the street your building is on. Thus, downtown areas or streets with densely situated large buildings can be challenging compass readings.

Many buildings and houses are oriented comfortably within the 15 degree ranges depicted in the compass illustration provided. Do an especially careful reading from several distances to compare if the compass reading is very close to the cut-off point between different directions. As Figure 3-1 shows, if your house appears to face 22.5 degrees, it is right on the line between northeast and north. Continue to do readings at various distances from the house and from both front and back, to get a consensus of the most likely reading.

Always do a comparative reading on the opposite side of the house or building. If the front of the house faces 90 degrees east, the back should be facing 270 degrees west. See Figure 3-3 for an example and for instructions on dividing the square quadrants within the house.

For most structures, the front and back walls are parallel and should appear 180 degrees apart in their facing compass directions.

If the needle of your compass does not settle down and point to one direction after a few seconds, you may have a faulty compass or you may be too close to some kind of magnetic interference or underground water. This does not happen very often.

Accurate magnetic compass readings are crucial. It is not good enough to just make a guess or estimate based on how the sun rises over your house, or on certain environmental landmarks in your area. For example, many people in the Los Angeles area incorrectly assume the ocean is to the west of them, no matter how their street is aligned. Looking at a map, the Pacific Ocean runs along the southwest, not the west, of much of Southern California. In many of these beach cities, a lot of the streets very close to the ocean are not running in a north-south or east-west alignment at all. Rather they are aligned northwest to southeast and northeast to southwest.

Additionally, it is always best to do a compass reading in person, and not just assume the structure must be aligned paral-

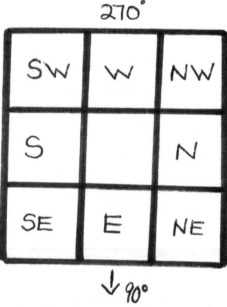

Figure 3-3. How to divide the quadrants of an east-facing square house.

lel with the street maps. Sometimes I have gone to do a consultation on a familiar street and find the actual property is not directly aligned parallel with the street.

CORRECTLY DIVIDING A FLOOR PLAN

Once you have your compass reading of the property, you are now ready to divide a floor plan into directional quadrants. This is based on your real and accurate compass reading. It must also be based on a floor plan sketch roughly (or more preferably, exactly) to scale.

Initially, chi can come from any direction and is not confined. Over time a house or building will give the chi a shape, much like water taking on the shape of its container. Therefore, the directional quadrants inside a structure will be much like the whole structure.

If you have a square house, the directional quadrants will be square in shape (see Figure 3-3). If the house is rectangular, the quadrants will be rectangular also.

Figure 3-4 shows a rectangular house facing southwest. The arrow indicates the facing side of the house. The illustration also shows how the directional quadrants take on rectangular shapes.

N	NE	E
NW	CENTER	SE
W	SW	S

Figure 3-4. ↓ If the house faces southwest, the back will be to the northeast, assuming front and back walls are parallel.

Obtain or create an accurate, to-scale floor plan of your home or business. Then divide the length and width of the building into equal thirds in order to know where one quadrant begins and another one ends. If the front facade of the house is 60 feet, each directional quadrant will be 20 feet wide. If the side of the house is 45 feet, each directional quadrant will be 15 feet in length. Other theories about how to divide floor plans will be mentioned in Chapter Seven. The quadrant grid method just described is one of the major methods used.

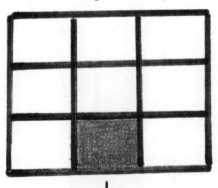

Figure 3-5. The facing quadrant is in the front-center area.

The facing quadrant is the one on the front side, middle shaded (see Figure 3-5).

The sitting quadrant is the one on the backside, middle shaded (see Figure 3-6). From now on you will know what a sitting quadrant and a facing quadrant are and where they are located in a house or building. Not every house is a square or rectangle.

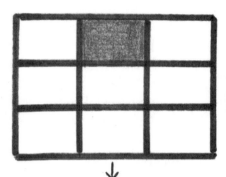

Figure 3-6. The sitting quadrant is in the back-center area.

FLOOR PLAN FACTS

● Look at the main *bulk* body of the house to find your square or rectangle. Many houses have extensions to quadrants and/or partially missing areas (see Figure 3-7). Figure 3-7 shows a house with a missing southwest quadrant and an extension of its southeast quadrant.

● Some structures do not have parallel front and back walls (see Figure 3-8). Although there are exceptions, usually take the back wall as your anchor to superimpose the nine-quadrant grid over the floor plan (see Figure 3-9).

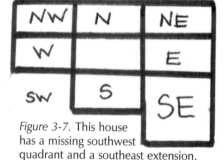

Figure 3-7. This house has a missing southwest quadrant and a southeast extension.

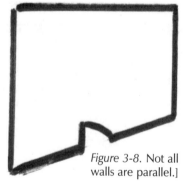

Figure 3-8. Not all walls are parallel.]

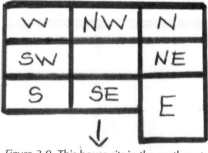

Figure 3-9. This house sits in the northwest with an extension to the east quadrant.

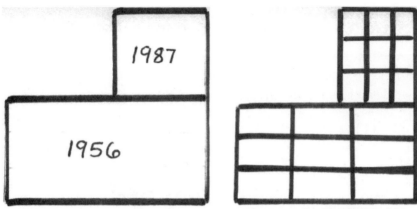

Figure 3-10. A house with a room(s) added on is like two houses joined together.

Figure 3-11. The original part of the house and the addition will each have their own directional grids (quadrants).

● When a house has had an addition built on, the new room can be viewed as having its own grid (see Figures 3-10 and 3-11).

● If a house has simply had an original room expanded in size, the directional energy will seep into the extension (see Figures 3-12 and 3-13). This is like a person gaining weight. Same person, just spread out more.

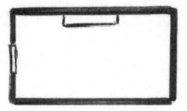

Figure 3-12. Original house without enlarging the room.

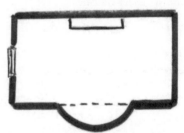

Figure 3-13. When an existing room is expanded, the directional quadrant just gets larger, forming an extension.]

THE ENERGETIC SYMBOLISM
OF EACH DIRECTION

Before trying to interpret house types with their various extensions and missing quadrants, first memorize or refer to the attributes associated with each of the eight basic directions.

NORTH (K'AN TRIGRAM)

Element: water

Image: deep body of water

Family Member: middle son

Number: 1

Body Areas: kidneys, blood, circulation, ears, fluids of the body (includes water retention or urinary tract).

NORTHEAST (KEN TRIGRAM,
SOMETIMES WRITTEN GEN TRIGRAM)

Element: hard earth

Image: mountain, monk

Family Member: youngest son

Number: 8

Body Areas: bones, muscles, hands, fingers

EAST (CHEN TRIGRAM,
ALSO WRITTEN ZHEN TRIGRAM)

Element: hard wood

Image: thunder

Family Member: eldest son

Number: 3

Body Areas: feet, throat, nervous system, liver

SOUTHEAST (SUN TRIGRAM,
ALSO WRITTEN XUN TRIGRAM)

Element: soft wood

Image: wind, traveler

Family Member: eldest daughter

Number: 4

Body Areas: lower body—legs, thighs, low back, knees

SOUTH (LI TRIGRAM)

Element: fire

Image: fire

Family Member: middle daughter

Number: 9

Body Areas: eyes, heart

SOUTHWEST (K'UN TRIGRAM)

Element: soft earth

Image: flatlands, sand

Family Member: mother

Number: 2

Body Areas: abdominal—digestion, elimination, the reproductive organs

WEST (TUI TRIGRAM, ALSO WRITTEN DUI TRIGRAM)

Element: soft metal

Image: lake, happiness

Family Member: youngest daughter

Number: 7

Body Areas: teeth, mouth, jaw, chest or breasts

NORTHWEST (CHIEN TRIGRAM, ALSO WRITTEN QIAN TRIGRAM)

Element: hard metal

Image: heaven

Family Member: father

Number: 6

Body Areas: head, neck, lungs

Now you have the above list to refer to until you memorize the attributes of each direction. There are other important pieces of information regarding these directions, but these are the basics to begin with.

HOW HEALTH AND FAMILY DYNAMICS ARE INFLUENCED BY THE HOUSE

When observing the shape of a house, if there is a directional quadrant distinctly absent there could be something deficient or someone affected by this missing area. Conversely, if the directional quadrant is an extended or larger area, it will have an enhancing effect on the attributes associated with the Trigram direction.

The northwest direction, for example, is associated with the father. If a house is missing the northwest quadrant, the father figure in the house will be weakened or absent. Sometimes this is a household where the children are not obedient to the parents in general or, particularly, to the father. The northwest direction is also associated with power and authority. In a commercial setting, the lack of a northwest quadrant will undermine the power and influence of the individual who is supposed to be in charge.

If the northwest area is larger than the rest of the structure, the power-authority figure will be stronger. Whatever is going on in the northwest quadrant may also affect any person who is the Chien Personal Trigram based on their birth date. In Chapter Six, you can refer to a chart that shows what Personal Trigram you are, based on the year of your birth and gender. This Personal Trigram is like a feng shui zodiac sign that is connected to one of these directions.

Figure 3-14. House missing northwest quadrant.

The one most likely to be affected by a certain direction is the person or persons who share the same Trigram. Example: a man born in 1958 is the Chien (sometimes written Qian) Trigram, which is associated with the direction of northwest. If the northwest part of his house is missing, he will be more affected by it than other occupants (see Figure 3-14).

The health factor is also considered. If the northwest area is deficient in any way, occupants of this structure could have problems with their head or lung region. This way of interpreting the directional quadrants is consistent with each of the eight Trigrams.

Eight Trigram Chart

	Body Area Problems	Family Member Problems
Missing North Quadrant	kidneys, blood, circulation, ears	middle son or middle-aged man
Missing Northeast Quadrant	bones or muscles	youngest son or young boy
Missing East Quadrant	feet, throat, nervous system	eldest son
Missing Southeast Quadrant	lower body	eldest daughter
Missing South Quadrant	eyes or heart	middle daughter or middle-aged woman
Missing Southwest Quadrant	abdominal area	mother, wife or woman in house
Missing West Quadrant	teeth, mouth, jaw, chest	youngest daughter or young girls
Missing Northwest Quadrant	upper body	father or authority figure, president or CEO

Sometimes the problem only manifests with the family member associated with the direction, while at other times any occupant could suffer the health issues associated with the direction. When an area is enlarged, the family member associated with that direction becomes more powerful. As shown in Figure 3-15, an extended southwest quadrant could reveal a woman in the house who, instead of her husband, is the boss and she will probably outlive him. A large east quadrant could make the eldest son more powerful, just as a large southeast quadrant could make the eldest daughter very powerful.

Figure 3-15. House with extended southwest quadrant.

AVOIDING PROBLEMS WITH CONSTRUCTION AND REMODELS

Aside from problems as a result of a deficiency in a house's shape, if there is some kind of environmental sha just outside the house or aligned with that direction, it will influence the energies and occupants inside the house. An example would be if the view from outside a south quadrant window is permanently ugly for some reason, such as a view of rough, gnarly-looking mountains, the eyes and heart of the occupants could be affected. This is because south is associated with the eyes and heart (see Figure 3-16). The effects will be worse the closer a disturbing view or circumstance is to the house. If you had a neighbor with a

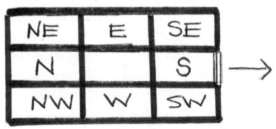

Figure 3-16. House with an ugly view aligned with the south quadrant.]

broken-down chimney aligned with the south part of your house, you could be affected by the attributes associated with south. For the neighbor, it would be the north quadrant of his house if it was aligned the same as yours.

If there were a diseased tree dying in a property's backyard aligned with the southwest quadrant of the house, it could indicate poor health for the woman in the house or poor abdominal health for any family member. This is because the southwest direction is associated with a mother or elderly woman, as well as with the abdominal or reproductive region.

There are many situations where anything wrong with an exterior environment will bring negativity to the directional quadrant it is associated with. It is all relative to your personal space. Your east is someone else's west. With environmental features that appear threatening, ugly, sharp, toxic, noisy or in any way chronically unpleasant, take note of what direction the influence is coming from.

Problems can exist inside a house as well. A crack in your wall or ceiling in the west quadrant, for example, could affect the youngest daughter or the teeth of any occupant. If you had water damage in the north part of the house, it would not only cause mold, but could also cause kidney or blood problems, since north is associated with the kidneys and blood.

You can take the information given about directions and notice the effects on a small scale in a single room. Northeast is associated with the bones and muscles, therefore, if a room in the northeast quadrant has a window looking out over a bad view, it could affect the bones or muscles of whoever uses that room.

You can take this same information about directions and superimpose it over a large area, such as a land parcel, and make generalizations about the health and well-being of the people on the land. I don't recommend trying to superimpose the directional quadrants over an entire country in order to classify such a large group of people. It would be meaningless to say people who live in a certain directional quadrant of the country are all prone to the same health problems.

HOW DO YOU REMEDY A MISSING QUADRANT?

Depending on what is practical and affordable, there are various options for correcting a missing quadrant:

● A good remedy is to enclose the missing area and make it part of the house, if it makes sense to do so. If you were able to enclose a missing quadrant and make a family room of it, this would be a perfect solution (see Figure 3-17).

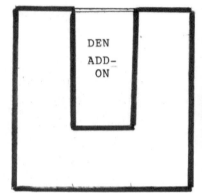

DEN
ADD–
ON

● Landscaping techniques, various plantings, hedges, gates and garden features can also bring a feeling of enclosure to a missing area.

● A person living in an apartment would have very little possibility of making changes to an incomplete structure or landscape. Thus, finding an apartment with inherently fewer flaws is

Figure 3-17. A room addition can enclose a missing quadrant or square-out a U-shaped house.

more important than finding a perfect house. In buying a house, there is more opportunity to make effective changes within the structure, as well as outside.

PROXIMITY TO CONSTRUCTION AREAS

If you are within a block of a demolition or construction site, the negative energy emanating from that area will make its way to your home or workplace. In addition, if you are remodeling a part of your own house, there will be an effect on you consistent with the direction in question.

This is called construction sha. Sha implies harmful energies that are directly related to the location of the construction site. This is yet another reason why knowledge of the compass is so essential. Avoiding or delaying construction within your own home during inauspicious times is the best remedy. Unfortunately, you probably have no control over construction projects outside your own property.

Neighbors on all four sides of, and diagonal to, your property is something to be aware of. You can be affected by the properties directly surrounding yours, as shown in Figure 3-18. Any of the following can result when remodeling occurs in a bad direction during a particular year:

● Accidents and injuries on the job

● Delays and hassles with the project

● The torn-up area can contribute to health problems for the occupants

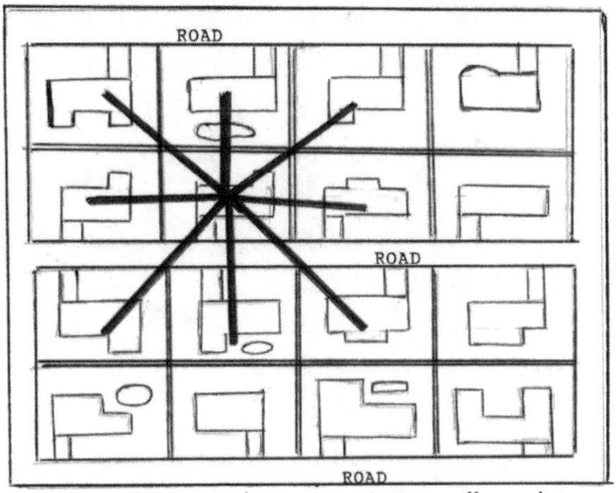

Even under the best circumstances, there can be

Figure 3-18. Surrounding properties can affect a house.

problems with a remodel that have nothing to do with feng shui. In those cases you must remember, the goal in feng shui is to go with the flow, not against it. Remember also, proceeding with a remodel during an inauspicious time is only asking for trouble. Figure 3-19 shows the precarious directions for remodel (or those to be aligned with) in certain years.

When doing a remodel in a bad direction is unavoidable, or if you are aligned with construction that you have no control in preventing, there is a remedy that should be

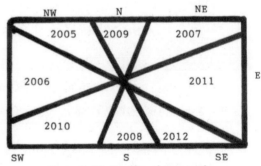

Figure 3-19. Tracking the annual destructive 5 earth energy.

employed. The negative chi generated from the construction site is considered an earth element. Referring to the cycle of the elements from Chapter One, you will find metal reduces earth and takes away its power. Therefore, the remedy to take away the power of the earth sha is to place a metal object between your property and the construction area. Much like a lightning rod, you can place a copper pipe in the ground to absorb the earth sha. This is one of the reasons why the Chinese hang wind chimes. The metal can deflect or absorb the negative earth sha coming from a certain direction (see Figure 3-20).

Which directions are bad for construction? There are roughly three directions (out of a possible 24) each year that are precarious for construction or remodeling. One of those directions is

Figure 3-20. If the annual energy is bad in the east, place a metal rod or wind chime outside aligned with the east during construction.

based on basic feng shui calculations for tracking the Flying Star Number 5. This 5 energy is associated with accidents and delays and the energy shifts directions each year. There is a repeatable pattern for where this energy moves year after year. In 2003, the 5 Yellow Star, AKA "the annual 5," is in the southeasterly direction. In 2004 it moves to the center, then in 2005, it shifts to the northwest. This 5 energy should not be confused with how 5 is interpreted in numerology, nor should you think the number 5 in your address is problematic.

Annual Number 5 Floating Sequence

2004 center	2005 northwest	2006 west	2007 northeast
2008 south	2009 north	2010 southwest	2011 east
2012 southeast	2013 center	2014 northwest	2015 west

There are nine directions (including center) and the annual 5 moves in the above pattern over and over. The pattern is center, northwest, west, northeast, south, north, southwest, east, southeast, then repeats (see Figure 3-21).

Another set of directions bad for remodeling or building is based on the Chinese lunar calendar. Each year is governed by one of the 12 Chinese

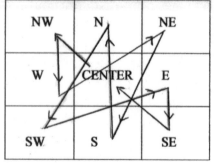

Figure 3-21. The repeating movement pattern of the Flying Stars goes from Center NW, W, NE, S, N, SW, E, SE, and back to Center.

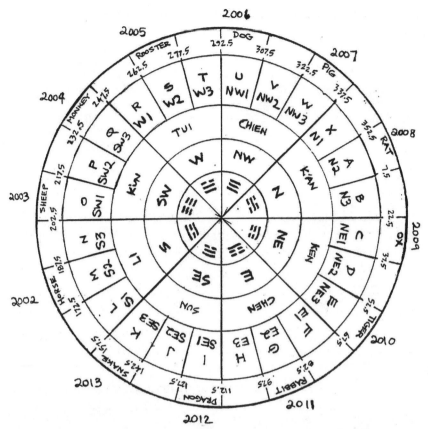

Figure 3-22. Tai Sui and Po Sui directions for remodeling or building.]

zodiac signs and each sign has a direction associated with it. You should avoid construction in your house in the direction indicated—or emanating from that direction toward your house—during that year. The opposite direction is also a potential problem. The Year of the Horse, 2002, is associated with 180 degrees south (see Figure 3-22). Therefore, south was a bad direction for remodeling in 2002 and north, being exactly opposite of south, was a secondary problem area. This can be equated with saying you shouldn't face the mean, volatile energy, nor should you turn your back to it. These directions are referred to as the Tai Sui and Po Sui directions.

Tai Sui and Po Sui Directional Chart

	Direction	Opposite
2002 Year of the Horse	S 2	N 2
2003 Year of the Sheep (Ram)	SW 1	NE 1
2004 Year of the Monkey	SW 3	NE 3
2005 Year of the Rooster	W 2	E 2
2006 Year of the Dog	NW 1	SE 1
2007 Year of the Pig	NW 3	SE 3
2008 Year of the Rat	N 2	S 2
2009 Year of the Ox	NE 1	SW 1
2010 Year of the Tiger	NE 3	SW 3
2011 Year of the Rabbit	E 2	W 2
2012 Year of the Dragon	SE 1	NW 1
2013 Year of the Snake	SE 3	NW 3
2014 Year of the Horse	S 2	N 2

Note: Directions for each zodiac sign have an exact 180 degree opposite direction as a secondary problem direction.

The cycle repeats itself every 12 years. Each year the bad directions shift 30 degrees. In a Rooster Year, the west direction is accident-prone, as is the east because it is the exact opposite direction.

On many occasions I meet with clients who are not in positions to postpone remodeling projects or are already in the middle of their remodel when I come to visit. Remember, this negative construction sha energy is associated with the earth element. Metal reduces the power of earth. Add metal objects inside or outside the precarious area before and during the demolition and construction phases.

Another footnote in the construction sha theory is to notice the direction of a new house being built. The Year of the Rabbit, 2011, is associated with the east. In general, 2011 is not a good year to build an east-sitting house. An east-sitting house is west-facing.

SITTING AND FACING

As mentioned in the previous paragraph, a house has an orientation defined by its sitting and facing directions. The sitting side, or the back of the house, identifies the real nature of the house. Think of it in terms of the human body: Your face is visible to everyone, but your spine holds you up. Therefore, the spine (back) of the house is more important than the face (front) in determining its real character.

Correctly identifying the sitting side from the facing side of the house is not always easy. It is important to recognize the front from the back, not just for the sake of these periodic construction circumstances, but for the Eight Mansions School and the more elaborate Flying Star School. For example, there are certain house types that need water behind them on the sitting side (this will be discussed in an upcoming chapter). If it isn't known which side is sitting and which is facing, the correct location for the water may not be known. Examples will be given in the next chapter for some very common house types that need water behind them. Obviously, books stating there should never be water behind a house are incorrect. Remember, there are exceptions to every rule.

We have an American expression to describe a person who is stupid or disoriented by saying, "They don't know whether they are coming or going." In feng shui, if you don't know your sitting from your facing, you will be ill equipped to make the proper adjustments. Sometimes, what is done *outside* a house is more potent than what can be done inside.

Sitting and facing can be partly categorized using yin-yang theory. The more yin side of a house is the sitting side and the more yang side of the house is the facing side.

YIN QUALITIES (MOST LIKELY THE BACK)

- Darker side of the house
- Less active side of the house
- Side of the house with the least windows and views
- Often the kitchen and/or bathroom side of the house
- Part of the house that feels the heaviest

● Side of the house or apartment backed up to an alley, back property line or another apartment or duplex

YANG QUALITIES (MOST LIKELY THE FRONT)

● Brighter side of the house
● Side of the house having the majority of windows and views
● Living room side of the house
● Where most of the incoming energy enters (road side of house)
● Ocean side of the house, if it takes advantage of views and proximity
● More open side of the house in terms of the floor plan

In some floor plans it is not completely obvious which is the facing side and which is the sitting side. The location of the door is often incidental, as with most apartments that have only one door. If the apartment is between two others, the facing side will be the one having the view. Think of the windows as eyes looking out (see Figure 3-23).

Sometimes an entrance door is on the side of a house or building. This doesn't mean the side where the entrance is located is the facing side of the house. It could very well still face the street, the most yang side of the structure. If you relate to the building as though it were a person with a face and body, it becomes more obvious which is the front and which is the back.

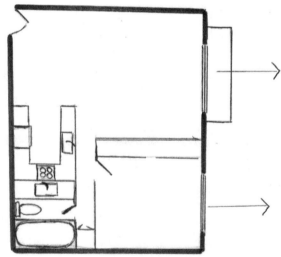

Figure 3-23. The facing side of this apartment is the window side toward the view.

You may have a floor plan that contradicts the basic principles. You may have a house with stunning views from the kitchen and master bedroom side of the house, not from the living room side. This is why each house has to be evaluated by its own uniqueness and why there may be exceptions to the rules. It also explains why two feng shui practitioners will view the same house differently. However, there really is only one correct orientation, about which two very experienced and highly trained practitioners will come to the same conclusion. For your own beginning efforts, if a house has the majority of characteristics to classify it as having a certain direction, go with that.

The sitting side of the house is sometimes called the Mountain Star Side and the facing side is sometimes referred to as the Water Star Side. This is just alternative terminology for the same concept. Mountain energy relates to people and their health and relationships. Water relates to career and income potential. Both sides of a house are important, but when push comes to shove, the sitting side of the house is more important. Referring back to Chapter Two and the house types missing their sitting or facing quadrants, this is one reason why the house type missing its sitting quadrant is a worse house type. We have the saying, "If you don't have your health, you don't have anything." It is also viewed as a person with a weak spine.

CHAPTER FOUR

TIMING IS EVERYTHING

The Shyung (Shoo young) Kung School of feng shui includes the Flying Star School. This school observes how the interiors and exteriors affect each other and the predictability of outcome is based partly on timing. This is the school that factors in the age of a building, as well as the changing influences of time. In other words, a house that had great feng shui in 1930 will not have the same positive effect on occupants living in the same untouched house 80 years later.

Because of this, I coined the phrase "astrology for architecture" in order to indicate the progression of events or circumstances that characterize a building. Using Flying Star calculations, it is possible to predict events and trends with surprising accuracy. In the previous chapter you were given the isolated chart for figuring out when certain directions are precarious for remodeling. That is just the tip of the iceberg when it comes to predicting how the timing of things affects us.

Let's say a building is prone to a burglary—it is possible to calculate the years and months most likely for such things to happen. There are even daily and hourly cycles, but if a remedy is in place for the yearly cycle, daily and hourly cycles may not affect it.

If a couple is trying to conceive a baby in their master bedroom, the changing masculine and feminine energies of the room can predict the likelihood of conceiving a boy versus a girl. Both happy and unfortunate events can be tracked. This is why feng shui, as a predictive art, has been grouped in the same categories as astrology and numerology. Scientists, too, make predictions, based on the amount of data available.

Engineers can predict, based on the structural components of a building, whether or not it will withstand an earthquake. In feng shui, we can predict what year, month and even day a building—and businesses inside—may be prone to certain dramatic events.

Although it's unfortunate for the reputation of the feng shui industry, there are no licensing standards by which any consumer can guarantee their feng shui consultant has had sufficient training. These are skills you are entitled to have in an authentic evaluation.

HOW THE YEAR OF CONSTRUCTION CAN DETERMINE GOOD OR BAD FENG SHUI

When a structure is built, the foundation plugs the building into the earth. The enclosure of the ceiling will capture the cosmic configuration and energies the year the structure is complete. This is referred to as Time and Space Theory. The timing of the construction and the space it occupies will produce an energy blueprint that can be tracked and interpreted.

I have inspected houses built on stilts hanging over cliffs, and not literally on the ground. They still seem to contain the same personality or attributes as those built on the ground. This must mean the energy from underneath the ground has the ability to travel straight up, even when the building is not literally touching it. This would make sense to all feng shui practitioners who know the energy grid on every succeeding floor of a building will mimic the first floor.

It is very gratifying for me to share this information because many consultants do not practice feng shui at this advanced level. Yet consumers are entitled to know the depth of feng shui and what they should be receiving in a consultation.

If a house or building goes through radical remodeling, it could change the original energy blueprint of the house.

TYPICAL RADICAL REMODELS
- When a major part of a house burns down
- When only one original wall is left standing during a remodel
- When a large portion of the ceiling is removed from the house

  Note: It is important to make a distinction between a ceiling and a roof. Every house will have a new roof replaced every 20 years or so, but if the ceiling stays intact, the original energy stays in the house. It is only when rays of sun shine down into a house that is exposed to the sky that a new energy is created.
- When a house is lifted off the ground to allow for a new foundation to be poured.
- When a house is moved completely to a new location.
- When the house is brought down to the framing on all sides and totally exposed to the elements (wind, sun, rain) while it is being rebuilt.
- When the structure radically changes its identity. An example of this would be a residence turned into a restaurant. Another example might be a church turned into a movie theater.
- When a house endures a fire so pervasive that every room is choked with enough smoke to necessitate new walls.

Some feng shui practitioners have less conservative criteria for re-calculating a house. Some believe if a new front door is installed, it qualifies as a new house. I tend to disagree with this. Also, if a house has extensive interior remodeling, this is like cosmetic surgery that changes the way a person looks but not their birth date.

By changing tile, carpeting and paint you do not change the inher-ent energy blueprint of the house. If the energy from the house was bad for the occupant's career, it will still be bad after the remodel. A differ-ence in materials used in the remodel, which can trigger previously dormant energies, may produce changes. Also, if the remodel causes people to use an area very differently, the occupants could have a very different experience in the same house.

An example of this would be if two small bedrooms became one large master suite. If the location of the bed changes, the occupants could easily be sleeping in a totally different location and/or direction than they did before, resulting in the house having a different effect on them.

Another controversial theory is called the Date of Occupancy Chart. This theory promotes the idea of a house's energy blueprint changing to match the current construction cycle of whenever a new occupant moves in. For example, if a house was built in 1950, but the current occupants moved in during the 1990s, some practitioners would calculate the house according to the 1990s construction period.

I have experimented with this Date of Occupancy Theory and found it to be inaccurate. I know from thousands of case studies the original energy of the house remains (unless there has been a drastic remodel) and will affect occupants similarly.

If I had advised clients according to the Date of Occupancy calculations, they would not have achieved the positive result they did. For the record, most classical feng shui masters agree with me.

Aside from these semi-permanent energies, there are also yearly influences that penetrate a building, coming from the various eight directions. Like a guest in your home or business, these annual influences will interact with the resident energies in the same way a guest in your space will either be welcome and a pleasure to have around, or a nuisance who can cause problems.

SPECIFIC ANNUAL INFLUENCES

Annual cycles shift around February 5th each year. February 5th is the midway point between the winter solstice and the spring equinox. Some people feel the shift in January, which is kind of a transition month for the yearly chart. Each directional area in your house has a single-digit number assigned to it, which represents the kind of energy residing in that area for one year. These numbers are code for representing many possibilities. In the previous chapter, you were provided with the Eight Trigram Chart and a number is assigned to each direction. These nine annual influences (in eight directions plus the center) will trigger or suppress the more permanent energies in that same location. Just by understanding the nature or potential of that one yearly influence, you can improve your life significantly.

LOCATIONS WHERE THE ANNUAL ENERGIES ARE MOST ACTIVE

Not every portion of your house is affected significantly by the yearly cycles. The rooms you spend the longest time in will be of utmost concern. Let us say that in this chapter you learn about a negative number (energy) in your guest bedroom or bathroom this year. It is really no cause for alarm, compared to more important rooms such as the bedrooms, office and main entrance.

In this next section, I will outline some of the symbolism associated with these numbers. They are, in fact, the Trigrams that were discussed in Chapter Three. They also take on unique meanings when they are annual influences.

It should also be understood that the definitions given for these numbers will change over long periods of time. You will be given definitions that are accurate up until 2024. A complete understanding of the 180-year cycle all the numbers go through is beyond the scope of this book.

After reading the meanings of the annual numbers, refer to the chart in Figure 4-1 to see where they are located in your house.

ANNUAL NUMBERS

Number 1. Power, abundance, prosperity. In the late 20th century, this number also had a negative connotation of being harmful to women. The 1 annual energy is becoming more positive now and this will last until 2064.

Number 2. Loneliness, bleeding, accident, miscarriage, separation, abdominal ailments. The 2 annual energy has been negative for a long time, but it will turn a corner in 2024 and start to become more positive.

Number 3. Arguments, gossip, robbery, legal conflicts. For most people, the 3 annual can easily manifest as arguments. When this energy combines with more serious permanent energies, there is a possibility for robbery, legal problems, even obscure events like getting bit by a dog or struck by lightning.

Number 4. Sexual attraction, sexual scandal, creativity, public recognition, academic achievement. The 4 energy has a dual personality in current times. The 4 energy starts as creative sexual energy, which can help actors and artists advance in their careers, but it can also create romance problems and infidelity. Knowing more about the house and the person potentially affected by it reveals whether the good nature of the 4 will come out, or the bad aspects instead.

Four, in Mandarin, is pronounced "sze." It sounds almost the same as the Mandarin word for death. Because of this, some Chinese people associate the number 4 with bad luck and will avoid properties with a 4 in the address. This is clearly not feng shui, yet book after book perpetuates this myth.

Number 5. Potential accidents, delays, arguments and illness. Between 1944 and 1963, this construction age was governed by the 5 energy. During that time, the 5 had only positive connotations, but those positive influences will not return until the year 2124! I find it interesting that the 5 construction period is almost identical to what we refer to as the baby boomer years.

Number 6. Power and authority. It is also a money number, but not as strong as 8. The 6 annual can be used as an example of how each number will react differently depending on what direction it is in during a particular year. As an example, the 6 annual comes from the Chien Trigram, which is the metal element. If the 6 annual is in the south in a certain year, the inherent fire nature of south would tend to dominate the 6-metal (this goes back to the Five Element Theory where fire melts metal). This could bring bad luck to the south. But 6-metal in the north, a water direction, could be generally more harmonious since metal strengthens water.

So, even though I am giving basic definitions of the annual numbers, different aspects of each number will come out depending on the direction it inhabits for the year. This is an example of how an analysis is layered with meaning. If you are a beginner, you are not expected to know the subtlety of these variations, but they are an important part of a professional analysis.

Number 7. A fighting spirit and ultimate victory. It can also indicate betrayal, cheating, robbery and violent assault. The 7 energy is a bit two-faced at this moment, considered unstable because it was positive from 1984-2003, but will now start to wane in its positive characteristics and change into its more negative nature.

Number 8. The best money number that will affect people most if it comes to locations such as the front door, office or bedroom. Since 8 is earth, it will be dominated (under pressure) in the wood directions, which are east and southeast.

Because the number 8 also represents a baby, this could undermine fertility if the annual 8 came to a bedroom in the east or southeast part of the house. South, which is associated with fire, would strengthen an annual 8 in the years it comes to the direction of south.

Number 9. Increased intensity in whatever is the inherent energy. The 9 annual may be the hardest number to interpret because it enhances both the good and the bad.

Figure 4-1 provides you with charts showing locations of the annual energies for some years to come. The cycle repeats itself every nine years (see Figure 4-1).

HOW TO REMEDY THESE ANNUAL INFLUENCES

In order to remedy these problems, you must first determine the likelihood of the annual number having a positive or negative result. What may be good annual energy for one person may not be for another. As an example, the 3 energy can invite legal problems, which is fine if you are an attorney, but not good at all if you are not. Then, prioritize its importance based on how frequently that area of the house, apartment or business is used. Below are some general guidelines for the numbers, without regard for what direction they are in.

Number 1. Since 1-water is usually good, you do not necessarily have to do any remedy.

Figure 4-1.
Cycle of annual numbers.

NW	6	N	1	NE	8
W	7	C	5	E	3
SW	2	S	9	SE	4

Annual cycle: 2004, 2013, 2022

NW	5	N	9	NE	7
W	6	C	4	E	2
SW	1	S	8	SE	3

Annual cycle: 2005, 2014, 2023

NW	4	N	8	NE	6
W	5	C	3	E	1
SW	9	S	7	SE	2

Annual cycle: 2006, 2015, 2024

NW	3	N	7	NE	5
W	4	C	2	E	9
SW	8	S	6	SE	1

Annual cycle: 2007, 2016, 2025

NW	2	N	6	NE	4
W	3	C	1	E	8
SW	7	S	5	SE	9

Annual cycle: 2008, 2017, 2026

NW	1	N	5	NE	3
W	2	C	9	E	7
SW	6	S	4	SE	8

Annual cycle: 2009, 2018, 2027

NW	9	N	4	NE	2
W	1	C	8	E	6
SW	5	S	3	SE	7

Annual cycle: 2010, 2019, 2028

NW	8	N	3	NE	1
W	9	C	7	E	5
SW	4	S	2	SE	6

Annual cycle: 2011, 2020, 2029

NW	7	N	2	NE	9
W	8	C	6	E	4
SW	3	S	1	SE	5

Annual cycle: 2012, 2021, 2030

Number 2. The annual 2 is predictably negative and as an earth element it should almost always be reduced with metal. Actual, weighty metal items added to the room can be a very effective cure.

Number 3. The annual 3-wood is not good for most people unless they are in the legal or law enforcement professions. Otherwise it should be reduced with fire. Remember, this means a large display of red color. A burgundy bedspread in a bedroom needing fire would be appropriate.

Number 4. As described earlier, this creative (and sexual) energy of 4-wood can be enhanced with water or reduced with fire (and sometimes weakened with earth to prevent infidelity). Unless you are honestly in the entertainment industry (artist, musician, writer, actor), you would not necessarily enhance the annual 4 with water. If you are single and looking for romance, you could also stimulate this energy with water, like a fountain in the room. If you are in an existing relationship, the 4 energy could attract outside flirtations and should probably not be enhanced. In other words, it will not make an existing relationship stronger or more committed.

Number 5. The 5-earth annual energy will be negative almost 100 percent of the time and should be reduced with metal.

Number 6. Be mindful of the 6 representing metal—if it comes to a wood or fire direction, there could easily be problems. Six in the east or southeast would require water to strengthen those areas. Six in the south would require earth to strengthen the metal. Otherwise, the 6 energy could indicate more power and authority if it was the annual cycle in your office.

Number 7. The 7-metal can be left alone sometimes, but for the same reasons as the annual 6, it may need to be enhanced with earth or reduced with water.

Number 8. The 8 annual number can often be enhanced with fire to create more wealth and easier fertility.

Number 9. The only time an annual 9-fire might need to be enhanced is if it came to the north, which is water. Since water can put out a fire, the fire should be strengthened with wood. Otherwise problems could arise associated with the heart or eyes.

An even deeper understanding of how to remedy the annual influence comes with the knowledge of what the permanent energies are. If an annual energy is like a temporary visitor to your house, even if it is negative, it can't cause as much harm if the permanent energies are balanced. This may be like a person walking into a room and trying to start an argument with people who aren't interesting in arguing, but who are instead calm and content. Examples of the permanent energies of common house types are coming up in the next chapter.

Once you have done a compass reading of your house, drawn an accurate floor plan and divided the directional quadrants, refer to the chart in Figure 4-1 for annual influences. This chart includes influences for the current year, as well as past and future years. It is often very interesting to look at past yearly cycles for your house to see if the annual number had its predictable influence on you.

Let's say the current year is 2006. Find the annual influences for that year on the chart. In 2006, the annual 5 is in the west. If that were an important room in your house, such as your bedroom, you would want to be sure to place a lot of metal in your bedroom, if you didn't already have a lot via the existing furnishings and decor. As well, you would want to remove any large display of the color red, because it would only make the 5-earth energy stronger. You can always refer back to Chapter One's productive cycle chart to see what element nurtures and makes stronger the element it produces.

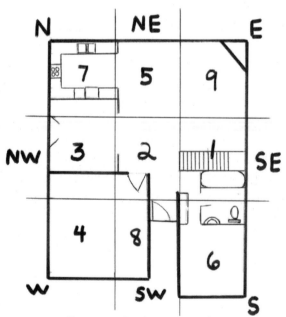

Figure 4-2. Southwest-facing house
with 2007 annual chart.

Just by learning about annual cycles, you could make some predictions about this southwest-facing house in the year 2007 (see Figure 4-2). The annual 8 prosperity is at the front door, which implies an increase in income that year. The 8 energy is also a part of the garage, along with the annual 4. If the garage is used as much as the front door, the increased income might come through some creative project or new business, suggested by the 4 cycle. It could also indicate a new romance or engagement for a single person living in this house or an extra-marital flirtation for a couple living in this house. The 2 energy in the center means the occupants may have more illnesses in 2007. With the knowledge of how to remedy these annual energies, the positives can be enhanced and the potential negatives can be reduced or canceled.

WHAT IS A LOCKED PHASE?

Every house will go through a period called a "locked phase." Some teachers call it the imprisoned star. Every structure has a major cycle that repeats every 180 years. Within that 180-year cycle, every structure will have a 20-year period where the structure is in the locked phase for money and a separate locked phase for people at another time. This locked phase comes at different times for different house types. One house type may have the locked phase occur within 20 to 40 years after having been built, while others may not become locked until 80 or more years after having been built.

Locked for People

When a structure is in a phase locked for people, the health and relationships of the occupants can suffer. It is a general prognosis for the house or building and it seems to undermine any other more specific information regarding the house type. As an example, if the house indicates a latent potential for heart problems, this is more likely to manifest for an occupant during the locked phase.

Locked for Money

When a house is locked for money, the occupants' financial endeavors seem to struggle more than at other times. These 20-year locked periods are something to consider when you are about to move into a new location. If you can avoid a locked house when it is at the beginning or middle of its 20-year cycle, that is one major feng shui flaw you can check off your list. But once again, this is not something you can physically detect when you walk into a house or building. A simple math formula can reveal which houses are in a locked phase or when they will be in the future.

A house will also go through a one-year money lock and a one-year people lock every nine years. Since they only last one year, they are not as critical as the 20-year locks and should not be the sole reason to pass on a house or building you want to move to. The exception would be if you knew for sure you would only occupy the space for that year's duration.

How can you tell if your house is in a locked phase?

1. First you need to know when the house, apartment or building was constructed. Call a title company or get the records from the assessor's office. I do not rely on landlords or property managers to provide accurate information.

2. Next look at the following chart and find the construction cycle associated with that year. For example, a house built in 1954 was built right in the middle of Construction Cycle 5, which was from 1944 to 1963.

3. Place that number in the center of the directional grid you have superimposed over your own floor plan.

4. Now follow a precise floating of the remaining numbers into specific directional quadrants. No matter what direction your house faces, the ascending flow of numbers will follow the same pattern: center, northwest, west, northeast, south, north, southwest, east, southeast. Memorizing this floating pattern of the directions will serve you in other feng shui calculations as well. If you haven't noticed already, this is the same pattern for the floating of the annual numbers.

5. Once you have all the numbers placed, take a look at what number is in the sitting quadrant of the house. The sitting quadrant is always the back middle quadrant (refer back to Figure 3-6). If the number in the sitting quadrant matches the number of the cur-

rent construction cycle number, you know the house is currently in a lock for people.

6. Looking at the number in the facing quadrant, you can see whether or not the house is locked on the money side. It will be locked for money if the number matches the number associated with the current construction cycle.

You can also use this method to note which houses have been locked in the past and which will be locked in the future.

Construction Cycle Chart

Built between 1864 and 1883	Construction Cycle 1
Built between 1884 and 1903	Construction Cycle 2
Built between 1904 and 1923	Construction Cycle 3
Built between 1924 and 1943	Construction Cycle 4
Built between 1944 and 1963	Construction Cycle 5
Built between 1964 and 1983	Construction Cycle 6
Built between 1984 and 2003	Construction Cycle 7
Built between 2004 and 2023	Construction Cycle 8
Built between 2024 and 2043	Construction Cycle 9
Built between 2044 and 2063	Construction Cycle 1
Built between 2064 and 2083	Construction Cycle 2

This pattern repeats through all the numbers perpetually every 180 years. Like the annual energy and the Personal Trigram year, the 20-year cycle starts with February 5th. A rare circumstance to be aware of is if the roof of a house under construction goes on in January before a new construction cycle. Such a house would be considered finished in the previous cycle. As an example, a house completed in January 1964 would be considered part of the 1963 cycle (Construction Cycle 5).

Figure 4-3 shows an example of a house built in 1949, which, according to the chart, was built in Construction Cycle 5. Therefore, the number 5 is placed in the center quadrant of the floor plan. Using the ascending pattern to float the numbers are placed as follows: 6 in the northwest, 7 in the west, 8 in the northeast, 9 in the south, 1 in the north, 2 in the southwest, 3 in the east and 4 in the southeast.

NE 8	E 3	SE 4
N 1	C 5	S 9
NW 6	W 7	SW 2

↓

Figure 4-3. A house built between 1944 and 1963, facing west. Money lock from 1984 to 2003.

If this 1949 house happens to face west, 7 would fall in the west-facing quadrant. Construction Cycle 7 is between 1984-2003. This means the house was in a 20-year money lock during that time frame. It is now out of the 20-year locked phase, since 2004 begins Construction Cycle 8. The house will not go through a 20-year money lock for another 160 years. Compared to other parts of the world, the United States doesn't have many buildings that withstand a full 180-year cycle.

NW 6	N 1	NE 8
W 7	C 5	E 3
SW 2	S 9	SE 4

↓

Figure 4-4. House built between 1944 and 1963, facing south. Money lock from 2024 to 2044.

If the same 1949 house faced south instead, you would end up with 9 in its facing quadrant (see Figure 4-4). This house would begin a 20-year locked phase in 2024 because 2024-2043 is known as Construction Cycle 9 (or Period 9).

N 2	NE 9	E 4
NW 7	C 6	SE 5
W 8	SW 3	S 1

↓

Figure 4-5. House built between 1964 and 1983, facing southwest. People lock from 2024 to 2044.

Using this simple floating of numbers, you can also see when a house will be in a people lock phase. Use a house built in 1980 as an example. Referring to the chart you can see it falls in Construction Cycle 6. The number 6 would be placed in the center quadrant and, again, the numbers would be placed in the appropriate directions (always starting over with number 1 after plotting the number 9). The flow begins with 6 in the center, then 7 in the northwest, 8 in the west, 9 in the northeast, 1 in the south, 2 in the north, 3 in the southwest, 4 in the east and 5 in the southeast (see Figure 4-5).

If this 1980 house faces southwest (see Figure 4-5), then 9 is in the sitting quadrant. It would not be in a 20-year locked phase until 2024! However, if the house built in 1980 faces southeast (see Figure 4-6), it therefore sits NW and was in a people locked phase from 1984–2003 because the 7 energy was in the sitting quadrant (the number 7 represents the construction cycle from 1984–2003 shown in Figure 4-6).

This chart shows a house type built between 1984–2003 facing northwest (see Figure 4-7). It will be in a 20-year money lock during Construction Cycle 8 (2004–2023).

W 8	NW 7	N 2
SW 3	C 6	NE 9
S 1	SE 5	E 4

↓

Figure 4-6. House built between 1964 and 1983, facing southeast. People lock from 1984 to 2003.

E 5	SE 6	S 2
NE 1	C 7	SW 4
N 3	NW 8	W 9

↓

Figure 4-7. House built between 1984 and 2003, facing northwest. Money lock from 2004 to 2023.

SE 3	S 8	SW 1
E 2	C 4	W 6
NE 7	N 9	NW 5

Figure 4-8. House built between 1924 and 1943, facing north. People lock 2004 to 2023.

Figure 4-8 shows a north-facing house built between 1924–1943 that will be in a people lock during Construction Cycle 8.

Now that you know the number associated with the perpetual 20-year cycles, you can chart out any house in any direction and see for yourself when the house has been, or will be, in a money lock or a people lock.

REMEDIES FOR ANNUAL AND LONG-TERM BAD CYCLES

How can you remedy a house in a 20-year locked phase? The remedy for any locked phase, whether it is for money or for people, is the same: The occupants need to hear and see circulating water. A pool in your backyard that you cannot see or hear will not work completely. A water fountain *in* your house will help.

Being a few blocks from the ocean may not be close enough, but a house that is literally right on the beach (waves licking the deck) may never go through this locked phase period. This may be the only certain good feng shui feature to houses on the Pacific Coast Highway in Malibu.

This locked phase is one reason why people do poorly for a certain period of time, then when the locked phase is over, life naturally improves. Even without knowing much feng shui, people who purchased all those water fountains (5 million sold in the U.S. in 2000) have been unlocking buildings and residences without even knowing why the simple addition of a water feature has improved their lives.

What about the annual locked phases? They come and go every nine years, but the remedy is the same as for the 20-year cycles: visible, audible water. How to tell if your house is in a one-year lock? This is where you need to combine the Construction Cycle Chart with the Annual Cycle Chart. If the construction cycle number you plotted out in the sitting or facing quadrant of a house matches the yearly number you placed in the center of the house, the house will be in a one-year lock.

Refer back to Figure 4-3. The number 7 is in the facing quadrant, indicating the long term money lock from 1984–2003. But in 2011 (see Annual chart) the annual number 7 will be in the center, so for that one year this house will be in an annual money lock. In 2006, when the annual number for all houses begins with a 3 in the center, this same house type will be in a one-year people lock just for that year.

Another example: Refer back to Figure 4-4. There is a 9 in the facing quadrant of this house and, whenever there is an annual number 9 in the center of a house (2009, 2018, 2027 and so on), this house will be in a one-year money lock. If you haven't figured it out already, it is possible for a house to be experiencing a 20-year lock and a one-year lock at the same time. This can be a particularly brutal year for the occupants. It is like serving concurrent jail sentences.

CHAPTER FIVE

ACTUAL CASE STUDY HOUSE TYPES

SPECIFIC HOUSE TYPES THAT CAN CONTRIBUTE TO DIVORCE, CREATIVITY, CRIME, INSANITY, GHOSTS, INFERTILITY, ROMANCE AND WEALTH

THE DIVORCE HOUSE

On the following page you will see a Flying Star chart for a house facing north, as well as one facing south. Both houses were built between 1964–1983. When either of these charts is superimposed over an actual floor plan, you can see where the directional energies are in each quadrant (see Figure 5-1).

These complete advanced charts have three numbers in each directional box. For our purposes, the numbers to pay attention to are the numbers on either side of the dash. You are not expected to understand all the complexities of these charts, but you can use them as a reference point. The size of this book would triple if I tried to explain how these numbers got to be where they are and how to interpret every single area. This is why people take lengthy, expensive feng shui courses and why a software program may someday be available at a store near you.

In each of the following house type case studies, I will be pointing out the more important areas to look at.

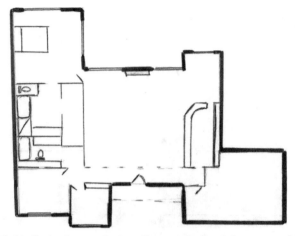

Figure 5-1. If this floor plan applied to Figure 5-2, the 1-2 area would land in the master bedroom in addition to being in the center of the house. If this floor plan applied to Figure 5-3, the 1-2 area would land in the garage entrance, compounding the 2-1 energy in the center. The center 2-1 energy can trigger divorce, but if an important area like a bedroom or entrance repeats that same combination, it makes the occupants even more likely to separate.

NW	N	NE
(1-2) 7	6-6 2	8-4 9
W 9-3 8	C (2-1) 6	E 4-8 4
SW 5-7 3	S 7-5 1	SE 3-9 5

Figure 5-2. House built between 1964 and 1983, facing south 1 (158 to 172 degrees).

NW	N	NE
3-9 7	7-5 2	5-7 9
W 4-8 8	C (2-1) 6	E 9-3 4
SW 8-4 3	S 6-6 1	SE (1-2) 5

Figure 5-3. House built between 1964 and 1983, facing south 2 or S3 (173 to 202 degrees).

According to Figures 5-2 and 5-3, what both house types have in common is the 2-1 energy in the center. The center of a house is the guts of the house and this number combination signifies 2-earth blocking 1-water. It can mean the woman dominates the man. If the man doesn't mind being dominated, the marriage can last. But most of the time this energy undermines a relationship to the point where couples separate. This is one reason why I call it the Divorce House.

To compound this potential, if the master bedroom happens to be in the other 1-2 or 2-1 combination area, it only makes it worse, since the meaning is similar. If you superimposed chart Figure 5-2 over the floor plan of Figure 5-1, you would see the master bedroom also has a 1-2 combination. If you superimposed chart Figure 5-3 over the floor plan, you would see the garage entrance has the 1-2 combination.

Obviously, this is an extremely common house and the divorce rate is very high. I see more people unhappy in this house type than others. I have also seen women move into this house type and find it hard to even get into a relationship because the 2 energy by itself can mean lonely or aloof.

Once in a while I see a couple doing okay in this house type and there is usually an admission the wife is in charge. Sometimes it affects occupants more physically than emotionally. The 1-2 combination can also contribute to problems with the kidneys, blood, circulation, ears, urinary tract and glands in general.

Remedy: Not all houses have the 1-2 or 2-1 combination. Those that do should have generous amounts of metal objects in those areas. The metal reduces the 2-earth and strengthens the 1 water. This is a practical, real life example of the reductive cycle as explained in Chapter One.

There are other house types that can cause divorce, but this is one of the most common house types I see regularly.

THE CREATIVE HOUSE

All four examples show houses that face various degrees of north, south, east, west. This Period 4 (another term for Construction Cycle 4) house has the creative 4 in the center. In all the examples, it shows how common it would be for a door or even a bedroom to be in the other "4" areas of the house.

Every house has some area or areas that can encourage creativity, but some houses are even more special in this regard (see Figures 5-4, 5-5, 5-6, 5-7, and 5-8), including all four charts and floor plan. Houses built between 1924 and 1943 have a head start over other house types because they were built during what is called Period 4, or Construction Cycle 4. The energy of 4 is associated with: art, music, writing, schol-

NW 1-7 5	N 5-3 9	NE 3-5 7
W 2-6 6	C 9-8 **4**	E 7-1 2
SW 6-2 1	S 4-4 8	SE 8-9 3

Figure 5-4. House built between 1924 and 1943, facing south 1 (158 to 172 degrees), with entrance through the 4-4 quadrant.

SE 7-1 3	S 3-5 8	SW 5-3 1
E 6-2 2	C 8-9 **4**	W 1-7 6
NE 2-6 7	N 4-4 9	NW 9-8 5

Figure 5-5. House built between 1924 and 1943, facing north 2 or 3 (353 to 20 degrees), with entrance through the 4-4 quadrant.

SW 9-5 1	W 4-9 6	NW 5-1 5
S 2-7 8	C 6-2 **4**	N 1-6 9
SE 7-3 3	E 8-4 2	NE 3-8 7

Figure 5-6. House built between 1924 and 1943, facing east 1 (68 to 82 degrees), with entrance through the 8-4 quadrant or back door through the 4-9 quadrant.

NE 5-9 7	E 9-4 2	SE 1-5 3
N 7-2 9	C 2-6 **4**	S 6-1 8
NW 3-7 5	W 4-8 6	SW 8-3 1

Figure 5-7. House built between 1924 and 1943, facing west 2 or 3 (265 to 290 degrees), with entrance through the 4-8 quadrant or back door through the 9-4 quadrant.

arly achievement and acting. You can see the 4 energy is at the center of each of these house types because of the period the house was built. Because of the way the numbers float into their predictable positions, it is very common for these house types to end up having the 4 energy repeated right at a centrally located front door (see examples of the

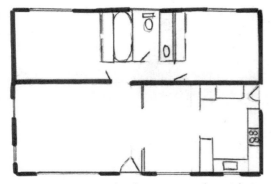

Figure 5-8. An example of an entrance door right in the middle on the front side. If this were a Period 4 house, one or both of the 4 stars would show up at this area.

north-facing, south-facing, east-facing and west-facing Period 4 house types in Figures 5-4 through 5-8.

Remember, the energy at the door is very important in the overall expectations for the house. Each one of these houses with a door in the middle of the front facade, has one or two 4 stars at the door.

Enhancement: What activates this house further is adding real water to the 4 area. When you purchase or make a fountain, have at least a few quarts of water circulating through the fountain. The more water you use, the bigger the result.

THE CRIME HOUSE

Whenever a house has the 3 energy in an important area of a house, or a 3-7 combination, there is a greater chance for the occupants to be victims of a crime (like a burglary) or for criminal activity to take place on the premises, such as drug dealing, prostitution, etc. The 3 energy was thought to be quite noble and positive back in the period referred to as the Period 3 construction (1904–1923). Now, some hundred years later, those same houses have changed their personalities. This chart shows double 3 (3-3) energy at the front door (see Figure 5-9). The interpretation is that criminal activity can come to this house or be generated from this house. For good people living in this kind of house, they may just be plagued with legal problems or gossip. Years ago I did a consultation for a record producer who lived up in the

NW 9-6 4	N 4-2 8	NE 2-4 6
W 1-5 5	C 8-7 3	E 6-9 1
SW 5-1 9	S 3-3 7	SE 7-8 8

Figure 5-9. House built between 1904 and 1923, facing south 2 or 3 (175 to 190 degrees), with entrance through the 3-3 quadrant. Occupants prone to legal problems, arguments, gossip or robbery. It also has a Construction 8 in the sitting quadrant, which means the house will be in a people lock from 2004 to 2023.

Hollywood Hills. He had this type of house with the double (3-3) energy at the front door. One time, a group of rap artists he was producing came to his house and assaulted him. Just to reinforce your learning, if you look at the sitting quadrant of this house, you will see the construction cycle number is 8. So this house will be in a people lock from 2004 to 2023. As another footnote, the master bedroom in my client's house was in the 4-2 north quadrant. This combination means that man will have lots of girlfriends or attract a lot of women. Not a surprise based on his lifestyle.

Years ago I did a consultation for a man who lived in a loft space in downtown Los Angeles. I didn't know much about him, but noted his work desk was in an area I calculated to be a 3 area. I mentioned he might want to move his desk because its current location could attract gossip, etc. It was only then that he divulged his occupation as a writer for the National Inquirer. We laughed and agreed it would be appropriate in his case to keep his desk right where it was.

Remedy: What reduces this nasty 3-wood energy is a lot of the fire element, red color or red lighting. What encourages it, is water.

THE CRAZY HOUSE

There are a few indicators the occupants of a house will be crazy or, at least, mentally unstable. Sometimes the shape of the house is so bizarre the chaotically moving chi will contribute to a crazy state of mind. The Crazy House can also be based on its indefinite orientation (compass reading). When the exact facing or sitting of a house is on the borderline between two different directions, this house type is termed "out of Trigram." It is like the twilight zone and the occupants will be very nervous or even crazy (see Figure 5-10).

Referring back to one of the compass points illustrations, you can see what the

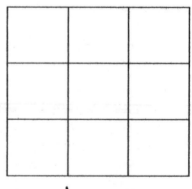

202.5

Figure 5-10. For a house to face 202.5 degrees places it on the line between south and southwest. This is called "out of Trigram" and is considered a house type that makes people nervous all the time, sometime mentally unstable.

borderline degrees are. An example is a house facing 337.5 degrees—it is neither northwest-facing nor north-facing, but right on the line. Very few houses are truly out of Trigram, but I do see this house type about 1 percent of the time. This is another example of why using a compass is so telling. Every degree matters.

One time I went to evaluate what I thought was a nursing home. When I got there I found out it was a boarding and care facility for people of all ages who were mentally disturbed, often violent and sedated at each meal. The building where their sleeping quarters were was an out of Trigram house, facing 337.5 degrees.

THE HAUNTED HOUSE

There are quite a few circumstances that can contribute to a house attracting ghosts. Exterior influences include being very close to a cemetery. The folks laid to rest and the other spirits who come to visit them are basically your neighbors in spirit and they may like to wander through your house. There is a Chinese slang expression for a cemetery; it is sometimes called a night club because the ghosts get very active at night.

Houses that are very yin will also attract ghosts. Yin qualities include chronically dark, cold, damp, built into a mountainside, overgrown landscape. Oddly, banana trees also have the curious ability to attract ghosts.

The people who lived in your house before you and events that took place on the property can also attract ghosts. An owner who died but who was very attached to the property could come back to visit. When a violent death has occurred, the soul can be so traumatized that it will not release itself from the earth's magnetic field or the spot where the death occurred.

Even wind chimes can attract ghosts. This may come as a surprise to feng shui enthusiasts who have been told hanging a wind chime casts off "evil spirits" and is a good all-around feng shui remedy. With certain house types, hanging a wind chime within close proximity to the wrong area can actually attract ghosts, instead of pushing them away. The sound of the metal only lures them closer. This is a house type that can only be recognized by more advanced feng shui practitioners of the Flying Star School. The 2-5 energy combination, with a wind chime added to it, can draw in a ghost. Here are a few samples of house types that have the 2-5 combination (see Figure 5-11). In Figure 5-11, the northeast quadrant has the 2-5 combination. If the back of this house had a porch and the occupant hung a wind chime right near the 2-5 area, they could actually attract a ghost. I do have experience with this being true.

In Figure 5-12, this house type has a 5-2 quadrant in the east quadrant on the front side of the house. Placing a metal wind chime close to that area is not advised.

N 4-7 1	NE (2-5) 8	E 6-9 3
NW 9-3 6	C 8-2 5	SE 7-1 4
W 1-4 7	SW 5-8 2	S 3-6 9

Figure 5-11. House built between 1944 and 1963, facing southwest 2 or 3 (218 to 247 degrees). The 2-5 area is in the sitting quadrant. A wind chime placed in or just outside that room could attract a ghost.

THE INFERTILITY HOUSE

Several components can make trouble for a couple trying to conceive. The house in a people locked phase is one such house. This house type will stifle the ability to add an additional person to the number of people who originally move into the house, therefore pregnancy is sabotaged. Remember, the sight and sound of clean circulating water can release the locked phase from a house and its occupants.

Specific to the bedroom (where conception often takes place), some bedroom

S 8-5 1	SW 6-3 3	W 1-7 5
SE 4-1 5	C 3-9 6	NW 2-8 7
E (5-2) 4	NE 9-6 9	N 7-4 2

Figure 5-12. House built between 1964 and 1983, facing northeast 2 or 3 (38 to 66 degrees). The 5-2 area is in the east quadrant. A wind chime placed in or just outside the room could attract a ghost. Not all houses have a 2-5 or 5-2 area.

energies also undermine getting pregnant. The 8 energy not only signifies wealth, but a baby. Eight is earth. Wood depletes or destroys earth. So if a woman is sleeping in a room where the Flying Star Chart reveals wood is destroying earth (8-4, 8-3), this could be contributing to the problem (see Figure 5-13). When wood destroys earth, the proper remedy is fire because it reduces wood and enhances earth at the same time (review reductive cycle chart).

In Figure 5-13, it is very common for this 7 cycle, west-facing house to have a master bedroom in the back left-hand corner. It is the northeast section of the house with the 8-3 combination. This is also a great example of how red color is sometimes very important to have in a bedroom. Too many books incorrectly state one should never have red color in the bedroom. Never say never; there are always exceptions to the rules.

Remedy: Add red color or lighting to the 8-3 or 8-4 areas. It is also important to not have live plants or real water in these areas. It would defeat the purpose to adding fire.

Another type of house that can undermine pregnancy is a house where the 2-earth energy shows up at the door or in the bedroom. Every single house will have two locations with the 2 in it. The 2 means potential for bleeding or miscarriage (see Figure 5-14). There is a 2-6 combination in the southeast part of this particular house. I personally had a miscarriage in 1990 when the annual 2 energy was in my bedroom. It was just about 6 months before I learned how to cure annual influences.

Two is earth and is reduced by metal. You do *not* want to strengthen the 2-earth. You want to weaken it (at least until 2024! After 2024, the 2-energy in a house will start to signify more positive energies, it will be appropriate to strengthen it only when it starts a long-term good phase).

NE 8-3 1	E 3-7 5	SE 4-8 6
N 1-5 3	C 5-9 7	S 9-4 2
NW 6-1 8	W 7-2 9	SW 2-6 4

Figure 5-13. House built between 1984 and 2003, facing east 1 (68 to 82 degrees) or facing west 1 (248 to 262 degrees). A bedroom or entrance in the 8-3 northeast area could cause fertility problems. The fire element (red color) is the remedy. A bedroom or entrance in the 2-6 southwest area could cause bleeding or miscarriage. In this case, lots of metal is the remedy.

NE 6-1 8	E 1-5 3	SE 2-6 4
N 8-3 1	C 3-7 5	S 7-2 9
NW 4-8 6	W 5-9 7	SW 9-4 2

Figure 5-14. House built between 1944 and 1963, facing east 1 (68 to 82 degrees) or facing west 1 (248 to 262 degrees). This chart has the same orientation as the previous example, but built in a different time frame. The 8-3 and 2-6 areas end up in different directional quadrants, but the remedies are identical. If this were an east-facing house, it would have also been in a people lock from 1984 to 2003, making it even more difficult to get pregnant.

Earth is weakened or reduced by metal. The proper way to reduce a negative force is to weaken it (reductive cycle). This is considered to be the more subtle solution than to dominate the same element.

Remedy: The bedroom that has the 2-earth energy should *not* have any red color, but instead loads of metal.

THE ROMANCE HOUSE

When the sexual 4 energy is in the bedroom, entrance or center of the house, it is easy for a single woman to attract male attention. It is also a good house for a gay man to attract male attention! To a lesser degree, it can help a man attract a woman. The 4 energy was just discussed earlier as creative energy and this is an example of the 4's dual personality.

Here is an example of a house type with a strong potential for attracting an exciting love life (see Figure 5-15). Remedy: To activate further, add water to the 4 areas. This is because the 4 energy is wood in nature and wood is always activated by water, like watering a plant.

(Figure 5-16). In Figure 5-16 it is another example of a house type that yields the 1-4 and 4-1 combination. This will be true for any building facing north or south and built between 1984 and 2003.

N 5-9 3	NE 7-7 1	E 3-2 5
NW 9-5 8	C (1-4) 7	SE 2-3 6
W 8-6 9	SW 4-1 4	S 6-8 2

Figure 5-15. House built between 1984 and 2003, southwest 2 or 3. The 1-4 in the center means there is always a potential for a woman to meet lots of men. An entrance or bedroom in the 4-1 southwest quadrant would make it an even stronger house for romance.

NW (4-1) 8	N 8-6 3	NE 6-8 1
W 5-9 9	C 3-2 7	E (1-4) 5
SW 9-5 4	S 7-7 2	SE 2-3 6

Figure 5-16. House built between 1984 and 2003, south 1. The 4-1 and 1-4 quadrants are in the northwest and east. If these are heavily used areas of the floor plan, it attracts more romantic opportunities. If this were an office building, the 4 areas could instigate more office romances, flirtations, engagements and secretaries chatting on the phone more than conducting business.

THE WEALTH HOUSE

Some houses are very strong in the ability to enhance the occupants' money luck, possibly for very long periods of time. This is based on when they are built, combined with their compass orientation, but the floor plan has to support this kind of house as well. Take a look at the two house charts here, built in the exact same time and direction. Both houses have potential for wealth, but one has been seriously disadvantaged by the floor plan in Figure 5-19. In Figure 5-17 there are two areas that have the 8 prosperity number and the 6 power number, in the south and southwest quadrants.

NW	N	NE
3-2	7-7	5-9
8	3	1
W	C	E
4-1	2-3	9-5
9	7	5
SW	S	SE
8-6	6-8	1-4
4	2	6

Figure 5-17. House built between 1984 and 2003, facing north 2 or 3. This is a special house type called a "Combination 10 House," and is considered inherently lucky. But the true luck of any house boils down to its actual floor plan, as shown in the following examples.

NW	N	NE
3-2	7-7	5-9
8	3	1
W	C	E
4-1	2-3	9-5
9	7	5
SW	S	SE
8-6	6-8	1-4
4	2	6

Figure 5-18. If the front door is in the 7-7 area and the master bedroom is in the 6-8 or 8-6 area, the occupants can do especially well financially.

For this house, aligned 0 degrees north to 180 degrees south and built in Construction Cycle 7, the 8-6 combination ends up in the southwest and the 6-8 combination ends up in the south. This is an example of how a house can have more than one wealth area. Then, it becomes relevant to superimpose an actual floor plan over this grid to see where the important areas land (Figure 5-18). In Figure 5-18, the master bed is placed in the 6-8 area and the front door is in the 7-7 area, which is also a strong money number combination.

Compare it with the house built in the same direction and same year, but with a different floor plan. In Figure 5-19 the basic chart is the same, but the bed is in the 9-5 area and the entrance is in the 3-2 area. These are two of the most negative areas of the house.

What is true for annual number remedies is also true for permanent number combinations. If you discover that you have an important area of your house in a 2 or 5 location on a chart, add lots of metal objects or furnishings to that area.

NW 3-2 8	N 7-7 3	NE 5-9 1
W 4-1 9	C 2-3 7	E 9-5
SW 8-6 4	S 6-8 2	SE 1-4 6

Figure 5-19. If the bedroom is in the 5-9 or 9-5 area and the entrance is in the 3-2 area, it is not as good a house as the previous example. In this arrangement there is great potential for arguments and accidents.

This is a great example of how potent and important feng shui is in the design phase of a project. The orientation and timing of when a house is to be built could possess great potential, but the actual floor plan inside could ruin it.

Virtually every house has the 8 prosperity number in combination with another number, as long as it hasn't been eliminated from the floor plan. As in Figure 5-17, if the south quadrant of a house were missing, the architect or builder could have unknowingly eliminated the major wealth area.

Other features that create wealth for occupants include:

● *An exterior environment that supports the house type.* A house with flat land in front of it and behind it is inconsequential. But some house types specifically need higher or lower land level in front or back, depending on when they were built. Examples of these house types are coming up.

● *Personal compatibility with the occupants.* Let us say you have moved into a house that attracts legal problems (see Crime House example). If you are a celebrity attorney, such as Johnnie Cochran or Gloria Allred, this house type could make you even richer and more famous. Personal compatibility also includes birth dates. More on that will be discussed in the next chapter.

● *A building type matching the type of business inside.* If you leased a building that supported fighting and aggression, and you happened to be a martial arts instructor, this building could help attract the kind of clientele necessary to succeed. On the other hand, if a married couple or young family moved into this type of house, it could sabotage all their personal relationships.

● *The immediate exterior influences* can attract shen-chi or wealth opportunities to the house or building concerned. If the structure is inherently good, the direction of the streets wrapping around the property or coming toward it can activate the positive influences even more (see Figure 5-20). In Figure 5-20, the street raps around the house (like the moat surrounding a castle). This helps collect wealth chi.

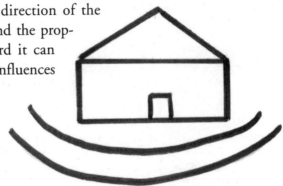

Figure 5-20. House where street wraps around.]

Virtually all novice feng shui books show a picture of a house at the end of a T-juncture, indicating this is an unlucky house. Not so, if the front door is the 6-8 or 8-6 combination. The chi moving directly toward this house will activate the 8 and 6 and make the occupant of this house even more powerful. The 6-6 front door can also handle the direct line of chi moving toward it. This is an example, where poison can become medicine.

Figure 5-21. House at end of a T juncture.

THE O. J. SIMPSON ESTATE AND THE ERIK AND LYLE MENENDEZ HOUSE

THE O. J. SIMPSON HOUSE

I was the first feng shui practitioner to evaluate the former O. J. Simpson estate for the couple who bought it from the bank. Several other feng shui practitioners came after me who agreed with my findings. As many know, this house was torn down and a new one built facing another direction. While I didn't personally insist the new owners had to rebuild, the original house had some design flaws that were difficult to overcome, and the new occupants wanted so many cosmetic and structural changes, it made sense to start over. Sometimes it is just easier to tear down than to remodel a house that has already had too many awkward remodels (see Figure 5-22).

NE **8-3** 7	E **4-8** 2	SE **3-7** 3
N **6-1** 9	C **2-6** 4	S **7-2** 8
NW **1-5** 5	W **9-4** 6	SW **5-9** 1

Figure 5-22. House built between 1924 and 1943, facing west 1. The 4 stars at the facing and sitting quadrants mean the occupant could easily be famous. The 8-3 in the master bedroom means the occupant could suffer from bone or muscle problems, including arthritis. The 5 stars at the front door and the garage entrance mean the occupants could argue a lot or have accidents and pain.

For Flying Star practitioners, the original house was one characterized as being generally good for people and good for money (Wang Shan Wang Shui). It was one of the better house types. O. J. did very well in the house, even until the bitter end. The house supported him all the way.

Philosophical sidebar: Can a bad man benefit from good feng shui? Answer: Yes. His ex-wife's condo is another story (I have to remind people O. J.'s house was NOT the scene of the murder). Some noteworthy aspects to his house include the fact that it had more exposed beams crisscrossing throughout the house than I had ever seen in any one house before.

Exposed beams tend to make people irritable. Though they may look nice architecturally, beams produce a real chaotic quality to the atmosphere in a room.

While some people may find it hard to believe feng shui causes anything, even the most skeptical person would agree a negative environment could be the last straw that pushes someone over the edge. Anyone with a migraine will tell you loud sounds and glaring lights can bring on thoughts of suicide. In other words, exposed beams do not cause a sane person to commit murder, but for an unstable person, they could definitely be a serious irritant.

Also, the master bedroom upstairs in the northeast had a Flying Star Chart, which indicated the occupant could have bone or muscle problems (8-3 combination). Having arthritis was one of Mr. Simpson's alibis for supposedly not having the strength to commit two violent murders.

Both the front door and the side door entrance had the 5 flying star, which can make even normal people argue and have accidents or get hurt. Even worse, there was red carpet in the 1-5 entry area. This color is an irritant because fire strengthens the 5-earth.

And finally, in Chinese astrology there is a certain direction for each person that is considered very lucky. It is called the Brilliant Star Direction. If you enter your house through that direction, you can become famous for what you do. For O. J. Simpson, he entered his Rockingham house through his Brilliant Star Direction. The Brilliant Star Direction can also make you very lucky. Under the well-known circumstances, Mr. Simpson was extraordinarily lucky.

THE MENENDEZ HOUSE

I did a walk through of the former Erik and Lyle Menendez house years after they murdered their parents in that home (see Figure 5-23). It was being sold by a couple without children who bought the house right after the murders. Some of the telling features of this house included:

N 2-5 9	NE 4-7 7	E 9-3 2
NW 6-9 5	C 7-1 4	SE 8-2 3
W 5-8 6	SW 1-4 1	S 3-6 8

Figure 5-23. House built between 1924 and 1943, facing southwest 2 or 3. 7-1 in the center means an occupant could be alcoholic or have addictions. 3-6 area was the location of one son's bedroom. The 3-6 energy means "the father can dominate the son." The other son was in a bedroom in the 5-8 area, which means "the son can have pressure on him injurious to his limbs." The 6-9 area in the northwest kitchen means the children will be unruly and not obey the parents. The parents' bedroom was in the 2-5 area upstairs, which means potential for accidents, bleeding, arguments and tragedy. The den, directly below the master bedroom in the 2-5 area downstairs, is where the sons actually killed their parents.

1. There is a kitchen in the northwest part of the house. The direction of northwest symbolizes the father figure and the element metal. The kitchen represents the stove and the element fire. In Five Element Theory, metal is destroyed by fire. The result is the children in the house are disobedient to the father—to say the least! In Flying Star calculations, the location of the kitchen also had the 6-9 energy pattern (9-fire destroying 6-metal). This is like a double whammy indi-

cating the father is in big trouble with the kids.

2. In the area of the house where the shooting spree started was the infamous 2-5 energy pattern according to Flying Star feng shui. This is the energy combination that can cause bleeding, accidents, arguments and disaster (not every house has a 2-5 area). The Black Hat practitioner would have incorrectly and arbitrarily misnamed this area the "wealth corner."

3. The parents' bedroom was also partially in the 2-5 area upstairs.

4. One son's bedroom had the 3-6 energy pattern, which can mean the father will be cruel to the eldest son. You can refer back to Chapter Two to glean more insight into the number patterns, since they are the Trigrams. The 6-metal represents the father and the 3-wood represents the eldest son. Metal tries to destroy wood.

5. The other son's bedroom fell in the area of the 5-8 energy, which means the younger boy will have a lot of pressure on him and could get injured. The 8 represents bones and a young boy. The 5 can cause pain and accidents.

6. The energy in the center of the house (7-1) indicates the occupants could have drinking problems or addictions.

Some other features stand out about this house, but the six items listed above were enough to convince me this house's energy definitely had something to do with what happened to the Menendez family. What was particularly weird about touring the house was the stuffy feeling inside. I have never felt such a tight kind of energy in an 8,000 square foot house, which normally feels airy just because of its size. It was also humorous to note the sellers had their dog locked up in a back bedroom during the Open House. The dog was barking like a maniac, snarling and lunging as I peeked to try to see the shut-off room. It was in a room in the 9-3 area of the house, which has a common potential to make a human being angry or argumentative or make a dog bite.

Remedies: If you think you live in this house type, even if the floor plan is not the same, follow the instructions below for the correct elements to place in each area. Once a place has been remedied, it can be quite stable for the occupants. Personal fate, you can be certain, had as much to do with their family tragedy as the feng shui.

> 2-5 area: Add lots of metal
> 6-9 area: Add lots of earth
> 5-8 area: Add lots of metal
> 4-7 area: Add water
> 9-3 area: Add fire (red color)
> 8-2 area: Add metal

The remaining quadrants need to be remedied in a unique way depending on who is living in the house. It is not necessary to remedy every single room in a house. In Chapter One, the priorities of the most important areas should be your guidelines.

There are so many other house types that match a wide range of scenarios one could experience because of them, but the sampling in this chapter shows just how personal feng shui analysis can become and how non-obvious these powerful energies can be.

THE FOUR MAJOR HOUSE TYPES AND HOW TO ENHANCE THEM

Even though I have mentioned each house is unique, on another level they all fall into being one out of just four major house types. This is a general, though telling, aspect to a house and once again is based on when it was built combined with its compass orientation.

First I will describe the house type, then give some examples of houses fitting in those categories. You should refer to the compass chart to see the degree cut-off points for the directions indicated. Example: S1—south between 158 and 172 degrees. It is also imperative to do a careful compass reading of your own property if you want to correctly identify it as one of the common house types listed (see Figure 5-24).

THE WANG SHAN WANG SHUI HOUSE

Generally considered good for people and good for money, in the big picture, this house type will support the occupants with their health, relationships and financial status.

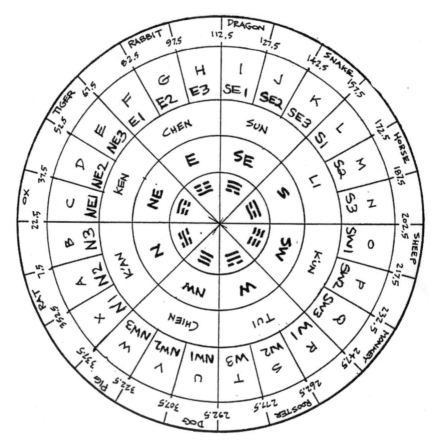

Figure 5-24. The compass.

Common Wang Shan Wang Shui house types:

- House faces south 2 or 3, built between 1944 and 1963
- House faces east 1, built between 1964 and 1983
- House faces southwest 2 or 3, built between 1964 and 1983
- House faces west 2 or 3, built between 1984 and 2003

THE DOUBLE SITTING HOUSE

Characterized as being good for people, but not as supportive for money, this is the second best house type because we are always supposed to care more about good health and relationships than about money. This is certainly true for residences, although for business locations, the money aspect is more critical.

Examples of double sitting house types:

● House faces north 1, built between 1924 and 1943

● House faces south 2 or 3, built between 1964 and 1983

● House faces south 2 or 3, built between 1984 and 2003

THE DOUBLE FACING HOUSE

Considered good for money and bad for people, the effect on occupants could result in a house where people make a lot of money, but are unhealthy or unhappy.

Examples of double facing houses:

● House faces south 1, built between 1924 and 1943

● House faces north 1, built between 1964 and 1983

● House faces north 2 or 3, built between 1984 and 2003

THE REVERSED HOUSE

Considered undermining for both people and money, anything indicated inside the house as a potential problem will be magnified in the reversed house. Some books call this house type the "unfortunate mountain star" and "unfortunate water star."

Examples of the reversed house:

● House faces east 2 or 3, built between 1924 and 1943

● House faces west 2 or 3, built between 1964 and 1983

● House faces east 1 or west 1, built between 1944 and 1963

Only some of the most common house types have been listed here. There are actually 216 basic house types, based on their year of construction and compass direction. They all can be characterized as one of these four major house types. It is also possible to have the main house (original construction) be one of the four house types, with an addition being classified as another house type. This adds to the delightful complexity of the total feng shui influence a house can have.

There are corrective measures for the double sitting, double facing and reversed house types and it has to do with the land level outside the properties as well as the addition of water features. Obviously, if a person lives in an apartment and has no control over the immediate exteriors, they are going to be more limited.

These four major house types do not totally negate other influences. If a person lives in a reversed house type (not good for money), but their bedroom location is in the most prosperous area of the floor plan, that is a great compensation and the house could still be recommendable. Please don't panic about your house if it is the reversed house type. It is a very common house type so you should not feel singled out.

CORRECTIONS OR ENHANCEMENTS FOR THE FOUR MAJOR HOUSE TYPES

The Wang Shan Wang Shui House

The Wang Shan Wang Shui House technically doesn't need any remedies outside, but by having higher land level in back and water in the front, it becomes a good house that is enhanced even more. This is why the simplified old school feng shui books generally state that the ideal house has a mountain behind it and a stream in front of it. You now know this is true for only one of the four major house types. Two house types should have water behind them.

The Double Sitting House

The double sitting house needs to have both water and mountain behind it on the sitting side (to make it better for people and for money). If a double sitting house had an incline in the land behind it, as well as a pool, it would be totally fixed.

The Double Facing House

The double facing house needs to have both water and mountain in front on the facing side (to make it better for people and for money). If the double facing house had a taller house across the street acting as a mountain and a water fountain out front, this would naturally fix it.

The Reversed House

The reversed house needs to have real water behind it on the sitting side of the house: a water fountain, Jacuzzi, pool—the more water the better. This makes it better for money. It also needs a mountain out front: higher land level, rocks and boulders on the front lawn, a neighbor across the street whose property is higher up and/or is taller than the reversed house. This makes the house better for health and relationships.

Having said reversed house types are extremely common, one should not be considered a death sentence for anyone who identifies their own home as one. Personal destiny still has a tremendous influence on what happens to you overall. I have had clients who were extremely wealthy who lived in these reversed house types, although they felt frustrated, as though they knew that something was holding them back from being even more successful. This includes a client who used to make $60 million a year and went into a depression the year he only made $10 million. It is always a relative experience.

Review of what qualifies as water outside a property:
- The ocean very close by
- A pool
- Water fountain
- A filled Jacuzzi, no cover on it
- Lower land level (virtual water)
- An alley or street with regular traffic (virtual water)
- A park (virtual water)

Note: Real water is better than virtual water

Review of what qualifies as a mountain outside a property:
- Real mountain or hill close to house
- Higher land level by at least several feet
- A fence or wall that is not attached to the house
- A very high tree, taller than the building
- Stone statue
- Big rocks or boulders
- A much taller building in front or behind

As always, feng shui remedies should be elegant and inconspicuous. Adding boulders to your property should fit in with the total landscape or design of your house. In other words, it should not look like Fred Flinstone's house.

CHAPTER SIX

ONE MAN'S CEILING IS ANOTHER MAN'S FLOOR

SUBJECTIVE ASPECTS OF FENG SHUI

GEOGRAPHIC LOCATION

There are personal aspects to feng shui that must be included in a proper analysis. What may be a good environment for one person will not necessarily be good for someone else. Many people naturally gravitate toward certain climates and regions, and the general location of where someone feels comfortable is an indicator of some personality traits.

● *Water.* Since water attracts money, the people who live near water often make this a priority in their lives and could in fact be wealthier than those in the same city who do not live as near to the water. Water is also symbolic of spirituality. Usually the hub of spiritual activities and meetings will be close to water areas. In Southern California, it is almost cliché to think about the spiritual types and celebrities who live in Santa Monica, Venice, Pacific Palisades or Malibu. Many of the most popular vacation spots available to the more affluent are also located near water. People who live near water are often creative and intelligent. The downside of living close to water is that it can make some people cunning or deceitful.

● *Mountains.* Since mountain energy relates to the heart, people who enjoy living in the mountains will be more heart-centered or down to earth. The only downside to this is that if someone secludes himself in the mountains and rarely ventures down the mountain, it creates a personality type that can be too reclusive and paranoid. I always get an image of a wild hillbilly trying to shoot suspected trespassers off his land.

● *Desert.* This is obviously a very thick-skinned, tough type of person who can withstand the harshness of the desert. There is a reason that the desert *is* a desert and normally it is not a good place for people to settle. With modern developments, however, a desert can be made inhabitable if adequate water is available. Las Vegas and Palm Springs are examples where enough water can balance out the harshness of the dry desert.

AGE

Children are in a perpetual state of growth. They are very yang creatures. Because of this, they can handle very yang environments, such as bedrooms, with really wild, vibrant colors. Teenagers typically identify with loud music and crave stimulating environments. As we get older, we usually seek out more mellow surroundings, colors and background sounds. What may be a comfortable environment or décor for a young person will not necessarily feel good to an older, more yin-type character. In this respect, feng shui theory will not rigidly claim one type of environment to be superior for everybody.

It is so interesting how some elderly people gravitate toward more yin environments, but overdo it. An example would be an elderly person who becomes a shut-in, never going anywhere and keeping the curtains closed. Such people allow themselves to be in dark, dingy spaces. It's no wonder they get depressed and sickly, compared to other seniors who migrate to hot, vacation-type climates, playing golf and enjoying their retirement with lots of travel and social activities.

GENDER

Though I am reluctant to stereotype, men are often less concerned with how their environment looks compared to its functionality. A stool can suffice as a chair and cinder blocks can sometimes serve as an entertainment center (and a beer bottle can be a paperweight). Women tend to want to beautify their surroundings, put up pictures of flowers and create a mood.

On many occasions, women clients have complained that a place feels sterile, cold or unfriendly when it really just had a minimalist, masculine design. Personal living space can mean totally different things to men versus women. Real estate agents witness this on a regular basis. A dream house for one person might be a house that feels like a private retreat away from the world, whereas the other spouse might want a house that is good for lots of entertaining.

LIFESTYLE

When I was a kid I had a few friends whose homes had roped off living rooms. The children were not allowed in the living room, but they could make a wreck of the den or family room. Nowadays, that rope is often invisible, just there psychologically. On the other hand, people sometimes have rooms that nobody feels drawn to use. It is not necessarily good or bad feng shui to designate certain rooms exclusively for certain functions. But in general, a house that is very large and only has one occupant will become too yin no matter how magnificent it may be on a mundane level.

At the other end of the spectrum, some houses appear to be overwhelmed with clutter and chaos throughout. Since balance is the goal in feng shui, a house that appears obsessively immaculate can be almost as uncomfortable as a house that is chronically messy.

The bottom line is you are the one living in your house, not your guests, and you should do what makes you feel happy and relaxed. If anything physically offensive exists in your environment, it will eventually depress your immune system. If your neighbor has painted his house a repulsive color, just looking at it will make you tense and, over time, will affect your health.

OCCUPATION

Depending on what you do for a living, your house may reflect energies that you need to have around you or to counterbalance your work environment. If your job as a special effects makeup artist has you surrounded by colors, images and props all day long at a noisy, chaotic studio, perhaps your sparse, minimalist house would be very therapeutic for you when you got home. This would also be true if you worked at a manufacturing plant or any business with an excess of noise or overstimulation of any of your senses. If your career demands that you interact with the public a lot, your feng shui environment at home may need to be more subdued than for a person who is by himself all day.

Another big part of personal feng shui, regardless of your age, lifestyle or occupation is based on your birth year. This branch of feng shui is sometimes called the East-West School (also known as the Eight Mansion School).

HOW YOUR BIRTH YEAR DETERMINES HEALTH ISSUES AND SLEEPING DIRECTIONS

You may have already seen charts, such as the one provided here, which categorize you as an east-type person or a west-type person or a specific Trigram. Your personal Gua or Kua Number is the same as a Personal Trigram. The directions considered good for you personally can be used to give you a winning edge. Take a look at the following Birth Year Trigram Chart.

Look up the year you were born and select the right column for male or female. If you were born between January 1st and February 4th, you must consider yourself a year older on the chart, since February 5th begins the new solar calendar for feng shui purposes. It should not be confused with the Chinese lunar calendar, which can tell you your Chinese zodiac sign. The lunar calendar vacillates every year by weeks, but the solar calendar always begins about February 5th. This solar calendar is used to determine your Trigram.

Year	Male	Female	Year	Male	Female
1930	Tui	Ken	1974	Ken	Tui
1931	Chien	Li	1975	Tui	Ken
1932	K'un	Kan	1976	Chien	Li
1933	Sun	K'un	1977	K'un	Kan
1934	Chen	Chen	1978	Sun	K'un
1935	K'un	Sun	1979	Chen	Chen
1936	K'an	Ken	1980	K'un	Sun
1937	Li	Chien	1981	Kan	Ken
1938	Ken	Tui	1982	Li	Chien
1939	Tui	Ken	1983	Ken	Tui
1940	Chien	Li	1984	Tui	Ken
1941	K'un	Kan	1985	Chien	Li
1942	Sun	K'un	1986	K'un	Kan
1943	Chen	Chen	1987	Sun	K'un
1944	K'un	Sun	1988	Chen	Chen
1945	Kan	Ken	1989	K'un	Sun
1946	Li	Chien	1990	Kan	Ken
1947	Ken	Tui	1991	Li	Chien
1948	Tui	Ken	1992	Ken	Tui
1949	Chien	Li	1993	Tui	Ken
1950	K'un	Kan	1994	Chien	Li
1951	Sun	K'un	1995	K'un	Kan
1952	Chen	Chen	1996	Sun	K'un
1953	K'un	Sun	1997	Chen	Chen
1954	Kan	Ken	1998	K'un	Sun
1955	Li	Chien	1999	Kan	Ken
1956	Ken	Tui	2000	Li	Chien
1957	Tui	Ken	2001	Ken	Tui
1958	Chien	Li	2002	Tui	Ken
1959	K'un	Kan	2003	Chien	Li
1960	Sun	K'un	2004	K'un	Kan
1961	Chen	Chen	2005	Sun	K'un
1962	K'un	Sun	2006	Chen	Chen
1963	Kan	Ken	2007	K'un	Sun
1964	Li	Chien	2008	Kan	Ken
1965	Ken	Tui	2009	Li	Chien
1966	Tui	Ken	2010	Ken	Tui
1967	Chien	Li	2011	Tui	Ken
1968	K'un	Kan	2012	Chien	Li
1969	Sun	K'un	2013	K'un	Kan
1970	Chen	Chen	2014	Sun	K'un
1971	K'un	Sun	2015	Chen	Chen
1972	Kan	Ken	2016	K'un	Sun
1973	Li	Chien	2017	Kan	Ken

With this Solar Calendar, each new year starts Feb. 5th

Figure 6-1. Personal Trigram Chart

As an example, if you were born in the year 1961, that is the Chen Trigram (wood element). According to the lunar calendar, it is also the Year of the Metal Ox.

This does not mean that one system is right or wrong. Both pieces of information are correct for different purposes.

Another example: If you were born, January 14th in 1957, consider yourself born in 1956 because the day falls between January 1st and February 5th.

If you discover that your Trigram is Ken, K'un, Tui or Chien you are a west-type person and, in general, you favor these four directions: northeast, southwest, west and northwest. Although it appears out of place, northeast is considered a westerly direction. There is a feng shui calculation explaining why northeast is part of the west group.

If your Trigram is: Chen, Sun, Kan or Li you are an east-type person and your favored directions are east, southeast, north and south.

HOW TO BEST UTILIZE YOUR FOUR GOOD DIRECTIONS

● Lie sleeping with your head pointing to one of your good directions.

● Sit at a desk facing one of your good directions if you interact with a lot of people at work.

● Work at a desk with your back to one of your good directions if you need to concentrate without interruptions (like having friends behind you for support).

● When lecturing or teaching, stand facing one of your good directions.

● Enter a house or office through one of your good directions.

● Gamble in Las Vegas or play cards with your friends while facing one of your good directions.

● Meditate in one of your good directions within a house or a room.

The theory behind this is if you align yourself to your ideal directions, many aspects of your life will improve, from better quality sleep to more success in business and negotiating.

What can you do if your spouse has the opposite best directions? Often, family members will realize they have opposite best directions. It would be ridiculous to create tension at home or work in the name of feng shui to try to reconcile the situation. Compromise is the answer.

If you sleep like a rock in a direction that is supposedly bad for you, make no issue of it. If your spouse tosses and turns all night in their bad sleeping direction, see if there is a way that he or she can sleep better in a different direction. Basically, cater to the person who is having a difficult time. Just by shifting the sleep direction, it could help them a lot.

Even though I incorporate the East-West School information in my consultation, it is admittedly limited and not the final word on how to arrange each room. In fact, if you own a business that you do not physically work at, you do not need to be concerned with personal compatibility based on your birth date.

YOUR PERSONAL TRIGRAM

Based on your Personal Trigram (see Figure 6-1), you will inherently have some weaknesses in regard to your health. If the house also indicates an identical potential health problem for anyone who lives there, *you* are more likely to have the problem than someone else.

For example, a south-facing house built in the 1950s indicates a potential problem with the heart or eyes. If you are a Li Trigram person (already prone to having eye or heart problems), your potential health problems might further be aggravated by living in such a house. This type of house would actually increase your chances of having problems. This is like saying if you walk through a dangerous neighborhood, you are more likely to be assaulted. When a person is incompatible with their own house, the chances of something negative happening increase.

The reality is that families are usually a mixture of east- and-west type people and it is challenging to always utilize your best directions. This East-West School of feng shui is admittedly limited and you should not feel bad if you are discovering that you can't use your good directions much. Do the best you can to turn things in your favor, but ultimately there are more important feng shui recommendations to be concerned with.

WHAT YOUR PERSONAL TRIGRAM INDICATES ABOUT YOU

K'an—
kidneys, blood, circulation, ears, glands in general.

Since K'an is associated with water, K'an people may be more creative, flowing and emotional than others. They may hide their emotions better than others as well.

K'un—
abdominal area, spleen, stomach, digestion, reproductive organs.

Since K'un is associated with the image of a nurturing woman, Kun people can be soft and sensitive. However, this does not conclude that K'un men are effeminate.

Chen (or Zhen)—
feet, throat, nervous system, liver.

Chen is the eldest son or a prince in the Trigram system and therefore it is associated with a person who can be very extroverted, like an entertainer.

Sun (or Xun)—
low back, legs, hips, thighs, buttocks, knees.

Since Sun is the eldest daughter, it implies that Xun people will be independent, a free spirit like the traveling wind.

Chien (or Qian)—
upper body, head, lungs, respiratory.

Chien represents the head in a metaphorical sense, and it indicates a person who likes to be in charge or the boss. There is karma with the head and lungs and I have noticed many Chien women who are smokers.

Tui—
mouth, jaw, teeth, breasts or chest.

Since Tui is connected with the mouth, I have noticed Tui people who are quite talkative, including clients who are motivational speakers, radio hosts or others who make a living with their gift for speaking.

Ken (or Gen)—
bones, muscles, joints, hands, fingers.

Ken is associated with the earth element, strong people, like mountains. I have also noticed a higher percentage of feng shui students who are from this group, perhaps because feng shui is an earth-related science.

Li—
eyes, heart.

Li people generally have a lot of fire in their personalities, walking, driving, thinking and talking fast. These fire sign people are a bit accident-prone, but somewhat fearless.

CHINESE ASTROLOGY

Chinese astrology is often practiced in conjunction with feng shui. It is more specific than the East-West School because it takes into account not only your year of birth, but the month, day and hour. This then reveals that each person is actually a combination of elements, not just one.

Using myself as an example, out of eight possible positions for one of the five elements (two assigned for year of birth, two for month, two for day and two for hour), four of my positions are earth. I have an abundance of earth in my chart. At certain times in my life, this will affect my health in a negative way. I can reduce the earth excess a little bit by surrounding myself with metal objects. Gold or silver jewelry would not just be for fashion. This also means that the metal remedies in my house are also good for me specifically, not just the areas of the house that need metal. Having an excessive amount of earth in my Chinese astrology chart can also explain my decision to practice feng shui.

Someone with an abundance of fire in their chart may become a pilot or an actor (or both, like John Travolta). Someone with a lot of metal in their chart could be a jeweler. Certain elements will prove to be very influential in our lives.

Although a very thorough feng shui analysis can be done without Chinese astrology, it is often helpful in determining what dosage of certain elements a person should surround himself with. As an example, if a room needs the fire element as a remedy, but the occupant's Chinese astrology indicates fire could be overpowering for them personally, less of the remedy could be used.

Chinese astrology is also insightful in determining the extent that feng shui can help. As an example, if a person wants a feng shui remedy for their house to attract a soul mate, but their personal astrology chart shows that they are destined to be alone, the feng shui remedy will probably not work. It might generate more romantic encounters, but nothing of any substance or duration.

ART

Art is also quite subjective. Most people have art around them that they personally chose and that evokes good feelings or fond memories. Occasionally, someone is obligated to display artwork that they dislike because a spouse or relative has gifted it. Just know that anything that bothers you visually will eventually undermine your health.

Pop feng shui books have done an excellent job in oversymbolizing everything, to the point where some single women are reluctant to put up pictures that contain only one person or thing, afraid that it signals aloneness. This is usually unfounded, but never underestimate the power of the mind. Once a suggestion has been made, it might be difficult to erase. Furthermore, what one person thinks of as beautiful another person may find ugly. Beauty is in the eye of the beholder.

When it comes to large displays of color, above and beyond any subjective feeling about it, that color can change the chi of the room. If you have a 5-foot canvas that is blue or black, it will vibrate the water element. If you have large displays of green it is the wood element. Large displays of red are fire and large amounts of yellow, orange and brown is the earth element. Metal is white, gray, silver or gold. When you have a variety of colors in a single piece of artwork or sprinkled around the room, they will cancel each other out.

CHAPTER SEVEN

REAL FENG SHUI VERSUS FAKE FENG SHUI

COMPLEMENTARY FIELDS OFTEN MISTAKEN FOR FENG SHUI

Describing the distinction between authentic feng shui theory and superstitious practices may be amusing to the skeptic who thinks that all feng shui is questionable. But as a practitioner, I can wholeheartedly say there is a difference and I am consciously obligated to speak about it.

Just because a person says their version of feng shui is ancient or from special lineage, doesn't mean that it is. Just because someone has a series of unrelated credentials and initials after their name, doesn't mean they have comprehensive understanding of feng shui. Just because someone's father or grandfather dabbled in feng shui doesn't mean they are entitled to call themselves a master. Just because someone has spent thousands of dollars in feng shui classes doesn't mean they are practicing it in an accurate or appropriate way. Evidence of incompetence is printed in some of the most popular feng shui books, where authors contradict themselves in one paragraph after the next, without even realizing it or without caring.

111

As well, there are numerous specialties, practices and belief systems that may be complementary to feng shui, but not feng shui by themselves. Here is a short list of some of the things people are doing in the name of feng shui:

● *Professional organizing.* I greatly respect the life-changing benefits a professional organizer can offer her clients and I refer clients to organizers regularly. Nevertheless, organizing and feng shui are not one and the same. In fact, a person could maintain a very clean, tidy and organized home or office while still suffering from bad feng shui. Some of the most popular pseudo–feng shui books are really just about decluttering and getting organized.

● *Interior decorating.* I am often asked interior decorating questions that will have little consequence in how the feng shui will be affected. Readers have gotten the mistaken impression that feng shui is about creating Zen-like Asian décor and that is not the case. At the same time, interior designers have skills and perceptions that can be totally complementary to a feng shui analysis.

● *Gardening tips based on the Black Hat Ba-gua Map.* There is a lot that can be said about creating a garden or landscape to benefit the house or building it surrounds. There were examples in the previous chapter about how to remedy the four major house types with land level and water. But most of what has been printed about feng shui gardening is not genuine Form School theory. The Black Hat method would have you superimpose the eight life station grid over your backyard and plant colored flowers to match the Ba-gua Map. This might look pretty, as any garden might, but it is not necessarily going to change your life. Likewise, patio furniture does not have to be wood or metal to suit the direction it is aligned with. Whole books have been written about this kind of stuff and if there is any truth to it, the subtlety of it is hardly worth mentioning. It is like an 800-pound woman worrying about how her nails look.

● *Space-clearing.* This practice uses rituals to cleanse a house when there has been a lot of sadness, illness, violence, negativity or haunting. Again, whole books have been written about this subject under the guise of feng shui, when really it is only a complementary practice. There can be both a physical and psychological lift from space-clearing practices (such as burning sage), but it cannot correct feng shui problems.

● *Aromatherapy.* I love aromatherapy and believe in the therapeutic possibilities of using essential oils and natural fragrances. However, it should not be confused with feng shui either.

● *Western color psychology.* Some feng shui practitioners use Western color psychology, not knowing if it is in conflict with Five Element Theory. For example, the color pink is calming and can evoke feelings of love. At the same time, it would be an inappropriate color for a room that shouldn't have even a trace of the fire element. Pink is a weaker manifestation of red (fire).

● *Life coaching, positive affirmations, meditations.* "May you live in very interesting times" is actually a Chinese curse because it implies the stress of war or any variety of social or political upheaval. Many people are stressed to the point where it adversely affects their health and well-being. I encourage doing positive things for yourself, such as meditation and long deep breathing. But these life-enhancing activities are also not feng shui remedies.

Some Chinese and Western practitioners incorporate Buddhist mantras (like doorway blessings), and it can make for a very exotic consultation, but this only alienates people who practice other religions and gives them the mistaken impression that feng shui is a religious belief. My clients who are Christian, Jewish, Hindu, Muslim, Sikh and atheist would be very turned off at the suggestion of doing Buddhist prayers or incantations as a part of their feng shui recommendations. I once called an architect to see if he had received my brochure and he promptly told me that he didn't "believe in my religion." He wouldn't even give me two minutes to correct his erroneous assumption. Anyone can benefit from feng shui, including atheists.

For the record, I have practiced two major organized religions during the first half of my life. Now I am happy to not participate in any religion. I have a personal belief—which I recognize as just a belief, not a fact—that some form of intelligence created this universe. Feng shui reminds me on a regular basis of the orderliness of the world. I also believe this source of intelligence possesses no human characteristics, such as wrath, favoritism, or ego, and is basically incomprehensible. When people thank their God for winning wars or Academy Awards, it just shows how primitive and superstitious most people are. If your child was kidnaped, then found nine months later, what part of that story involved God? Echoing the rants of comedic commentator Dennis Miller, "It's just my opinion, I could be wrong."

● *Dowsing, geopathic stress testing.* This is a whole other practice unto itself where there can be interesting parallels to feng shui. Ironically, a lot of major cities have been built over ley lines and the cross points of negative earth energy grids. Some people also correlate underground water and electrical fields with serious health problems.

● *Natural house construction and ergonomics.* These are very complementary to feng shui, but separate fields.

● *Wardrobe and hairstyle consulting.* This is nothing more than feng shui marketing gimmicks at their worst. It takes the words "feng shui," which imply balance, and stretches them way beyond their intended scope. It is like the word "guru," which literally means the "vehicle that takes you from darkness to light." For hundreds of years it was used as a title for a spiritual teacher. Nowadays it's been diluted to simply convey a so-called expert in any field, such as "the gurus of Wall Street." You can't feng shui a car either.

● *Astrology.* Not only do people blend Chinese astrology with feng shui, there are even a few people who are blending Western astrology with feng shui. This doesn't make sense because Western astrology does not use the same elements as feng shui. Astrology can tell you about your personality, strengths and weaknesses. It can tell you in a progressive chart the things that might happen to you in any given year, and people frequently use astrology to determine compatibility with another person. It is even possible for an astrologer to do a chart for places and events, not just for people. As an example, an astrologer can do a chart for when a business incorporates, for when a country establishes its existence, when two people combine their destinies with a wedding date, etc. But astrology does not predict how you are affected by your immediate environment. This is why Chinese astrology was practiced in conjunction with feng shui and why Vedic (Indian) astrology was practiced alongside Vaastu Shastra (the Indian version of feng shui).

POPULAR MYTHS AND SUPERSTITIONS

Following is a list of some of the more annoying placebos, lies, superstitions or misinterpreted feng shui cures:

- **Wind chimes.** Originating as a moving metal remedy, they are now used indiscriminately as a lucky item to chime away negative spirits. In a location that doesn't need a metal remedy, they could actually cause harm.

- **Bamboo flutes.** The ritual of hanging bamboo flutes on exposed beams does not correct the architectural, energetic problem. If anything, it makes the beams more conspicuous. The notion behind this maintains that air passes through the flutes to help uplift the oppressive weight of exposed beams. Also ridiculous: hanging Chinese firecrackers to symbolically explode the beams. This was actually printed years ago in the *Los Angeles Times* in a feng shui advice column.

- **Live bamboo plants.** Since the bamboo is such a hardy plant, it symbolizes long life. Yet, it is not an essential item to have in your home. As well, various other plants and flowers may have metaphorical connotations, but they are not required in order for your home to have good feng shui.

- **Hanging crystals.** This is a purely a new age variation of the wind chime. Glass crystals hanging from the ceiling may in fact slow down the air currents between two windows or doors, but they do not by themselves balance or purify a room. Of all the homes I visit where glass crystals are hanging, I rarely see the justification for them. They do create nice rainbows, however.

● *Chinese banners.* Hanging Chinese calligraphy and artwork can be a nice decorative touch if they happen to look good with your décor. Not a feng shui remedy.

● *Having a television in your bedroom.* The New Age interpretation of the idiot box is that it is somehow an unacceptable presence in the bedroom. Energy-wise, its magnetic field is not good to be close to for long periods. But as far as symbolism is concerned, the television should *not* be considered partner to George Bush's "axis of evil."

● *You lose your wealth through your toilet.* This is another popular Black Hat School invention. It is my belief, wealth can only be lost through a toilet as the result of a last-ditch effort to avoid a drug bust. Besides, rich people have more toilets than poor people! Think about it.

● *Animal figurines.* There must be a whole Noah's Ark full of animals that symbolize various positive attributes that people are trying to attain or maintain in their lives. Again, these figurines and knick-knacks may be harmless decorative objects that bring beauty or whimsy to your home, but they should not be taken seriously as feng shui corrective cures. The long list of lucky animals includes turtles, fish, various birds, lions, elephants, Fu dogs, dragons and all the animals representative of the Chinese zodiac signs. Books are filled with the particulars of placing a certain number and color of fish to use in an aquarium. The trunk-up elephant purportedly attracts wealth if placed in various directions and positions. Lion statues with their paws outstretched supposedly protect the building they sit in front of, but to the detriment of the establishments across the street.

Just remember that statuary and figurines fall into the subjective category of art. If looking at a statue of Buddha or a frog with a coin in its mouth makes you feel good, more power to you, but they are not to be confused with substantial remedies. If a Mickey Mouse poster makes you feel good, I guess that is just as valid.

● *Placing a pair of Mandarin ducks in southwest for love.* It is true that some birds and ducks are more monogamous than humans, but placing an image of them in the home is not a guarantee that you will attract a serious life partner. Only one thing is for certain: Having tons of knickknacks in your home will definitely collect dust.

● *Chinese gold coins.* Any images of money can have a placebo effect. But logically speaking, American money would seem like the most powerfully suggestive currency to use if you are going to use money at all. Originally, Chinese gold coins were used as a convenient metal remedy. Instead of lacing your doorway with Chinese Gold coins, a hefty iron entry table would be more effective, if you really needed metal there.

● *Painting your door red.* This is one of the most haphazard practices. A lot of red color vibrates the fire element and most of the time it is incorrect to paint a door red, including doors that face south. There is a common myth that doors in the south should be red, but this is harmful most of the time. Flying Star practitioners know why this is so.

● *Placing a Ba-gua mirror over a doorway.* The Ba-gua mirror is octagonal in shape and usually has the feng shui Trigram symbols printed on the perimeter. Like hanging a Mezuzah at the door in a Jewish home, the Ba-gua mirror is supposed to protect the home and deflect away negative spirits. It would be nice if the Ba-gua mirror could drive away proselytizing Jehovah's Witnesses, but I do not think the Ba-gua mirror has the power to do anything. Master Sang once said they are just like a banner that says, "I'm worried I have bad feng shui."

● *Placing a mirror behind the kitchen stove.* This one is supposed to bring wealth to your family. It comes from the superstition that if the mirror reflects twice as much food preparation, you are wealthy by virtue of being able to feed more people. In reality, the mirror behind the stove will only reveal whether or not you are on a low-fat diet based on the amount of grease that splatters onto it. Or with the same train of thought, if you have a mirror in your bedroom that reflects you and your lover having sex, does this mean you wish to bring another couple into your bedroom?

● *A garage under a bedroom spells disaster.* Not according to my experience. Nor is there 6,000 years' worth of documentation for studying the effects of parking a car inside the house.

● *If the land drops off behind your house, it means you won't have any sons.* First of all, the reversed house type described in earlier chapters actually needs lower land level (virtual water) behind it to make it better for prosperity. Secondly, based on the concepts of sitting and facing, it is also possible that the house faces the views, so the drop-off behind the house might in fact be the front of the house and not the back at all. I have encountered this situation a number of times where a house with good feng shui was superficially dismissed by a novice for this reason alone.

● *Right direction, wrong element.* There is also a whole new group of feng shui adherents who call themselves Compass School practitioners who do not use the compass or elements properly. They do in fact show up for jobs, compass in hand, to determine the real directions for each part of the floor plan. They automatically assign certain colors and elements to those directions, without taking into consideration any other data that supersedes the basic eight directions.

As an example, north is associated with water, but this does not mean everyone should place a water fountain in the north part of their house. East is associated with the wood element, but that does not mean that the east part of your house should be packed with plants or painted green. The proper distribution of the elements will vary depending on when the house was constructed. This should be very apparent when reviewing the case study examples in this book.

● *Dried flowers.* The myth is that they represent death and decay. Actually, they are no deader than wood furnishings. Feel free to have dried flower arrangements, especially dried bouquets preserved from such happy events as weddings and showers.

● *Storing things under your bed.* This lie is very annoying because sometimes the entire bed takes up a directional quadrant that needs a remedy and the only place to put the remedy is under the bed (usually metal). For some, it really helps save space in a tiny apartment, by using the area under the bed for storage. I would like to go on record as saying that unless you are keeping dead bodies under your bed, it is a perfectly acceptable area to use for storage.

● **When a fish in your tank dies.** The lie is that this poor fish somehow died for your sins or that it absorbed negativity in the house, the way a sponge can mop up a spill. I believe this to be nonsense and just indicative of not cleaning your tank properly or neglecting the proper care of your fish.

● **Keeping books in your bedroom.** This lie would have you believe that if you keep books in your room, you will be overly stimulated and not able to sleep well. This comes from the same group of people who think that if you have an exercise bike or a treadmill in your bedroom you will be working out too hard to find a satisfactory love relationship. Unfortunately, it is this kind of psychobabble that pervades New Age feng shui and diminishes the credibility of all the remedies and theories.

● **Antiques.** The New Age interpretation of antiques is that they are prone to storing negative energy from the past or from a negative previous owner. This is not necessarily true and all antiques should not be banned from your possession because of it.

● **Addresses with the number 4.** The word "four" in Mandarin is "sze." It sounds almost like their word for death. So there is a feeling among Chinese that 4 is an unlucky number. It actually has nothing to do with feng shui, yet there are both Asians and Americans who shy away from a house with a 4 in the address or the fourth floor of a building. This may be equivalent to Americans thinking 13 is an unlucky number. Yet, in feng shui Trigram theory, the 4 energy is actually associated with romance, travel, scholastic achievement and the arts (as described in various case study examples).

● **Skylights.** This is supposedly bad feng shui because of the fear that the chi from the room can leak away. In my experience this is not true.

ONE HOUSE, THREE STYLES OF INTERPRETATION

What follows is an example of how three different schools of feng shui will diagnose differently and prescribe differently for the same house.

The house depicted in Figure 7-1 faces northwest at 315 degrees and was built in 1950. The floor plan is one of 216 basic charts, based on orientation and the time frame it was built.

CASE STUDY #1

Black Hat School. The Black Hat School (see Figure 7-2) pays no attention to actual compass directions and always assigns the back right-hand corner of the house to be a marriage or partnership area.

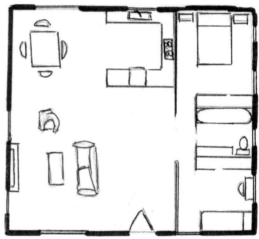

Figure 7-1. House facing northwest 315 degrees. Refer to in following examples, comparing four different interpretations.

Their interpretation might be how auspicious it is that a bedroom is located there. Recommendations for red and pink colors might be given for this room since the Black Hat borrows from Western color psychology and interprets these colors as promoting love.

The front door is in the imaginary career station, which they say is always in the front center location according to the comical BTB Ba-gua Map. Since careers need to flow, or be stimulated, a Black Hat person would recommend water for that location. Next, since the Black Hat School considers the back middle part of every house as a fame area, their recommendation is to place red color there to fire it up.

None of these recommendations would be correct from a traditional per-

Wealth	Fame	Marriage
Family	Health	Children
Wisdom	Career	Helpful People

Figure 7-2. Black Hat School. This New Age Ba-gua is superimposed on every floor plan.

spective. Referring to the Flying Star Chart (Figure 7-3), the trilogy of numbers in each directional box is code for the unseen influences of the room.

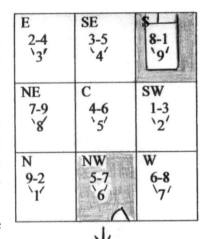

E 2-4 \3/	SE 3-5 \4/	S 8-1 \9/
NE 7-9 \8/	C 4-6 \5/	SW 1-3 \2/
N 9-2 \1/	NW 5-7 \6/	W 6-8 \7/

Figure 7-3. Flying Star School Chart for 1950s house, facing 315 degrees northwest.

- Adding red color in this back right-hand room could contribute to circulation or kidney problems (see Figure 7-3). The 8-1 combination indicates a potential for health problems in this area.

- Water at this particular (5-7) entrance in the northwest could undermine financial success since water reduces metal and it is the 7 metal that has been supportive for money during 1984–2003 and will continue to be a money number for a while longer. Since water will stimulate whatever is around, placing it in a 5 area is only done in special circumstances.

- Red color in the 3-5 back middle area could cause accidents or arguments for the family members, particularly a son. In fact, in the particular example given, the use of the stove in the kitchen could ignite that problem without the addition of red color.

New Age Compass School. The New Age Compass School (see Figure 7-4) is just as overly simplistic as the Black Hat School. Elements are rigidly assigned to certain directions, regardless of when the structure was built.

The chart (see Figure 7-4) shows the arbitrary assignment of elements to this floor plan, based on the inherent element associated with the direction. This was covered in Chapter Three. A Compass School novice would automatically recommend these elements and their

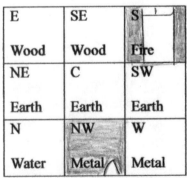

E Wood	SE Wood	S Fire
NE Earth	C Earth	SW Earth
N Water	NW Metal	W Metal

Figure 7-4. The abbreviated Compass School arbitrarily assigns elements to certain directions without factoring in the age of the structure.

associated colors for each part of the house, not knowing that the aspect of time makes everything move around. From the perspective of the Flying Star School, only two out of the nine areas would have been corrected with the proper element—and by accident.

Often, the Compass people combine the Black Hat Ba-gua Map and superimpose it over their directional chart, or they identify the imaginary career area wherever north actually is, with all the other life stations following suit. Master Sang refers to this hodgepodge style of feng shui as "chop suey." It is basically a mistake on top of a mistake.

Flying Star School. Taking note of the number pattern throughout the floor plan chart (see Figure 7-3), each quadrant has a sequence of numbers that flows from the sitting number to the construction cycle number to the facing number (see Figure 7-5). Example: The east quadrant has a sequence of 2-3-4. The southeast quadrant has a sequence of 3-4-5. The southwest quadrant has a sequence of 1-2-3. Each directional quadrant has a sequential arrangement of numbers. This arrangement of the numbers does not happen very often. This is a special circumstance house called "string of pearls." Sounds good, but it isn't.

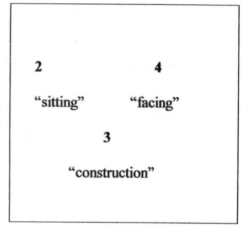

Figure 7-5. The Flying Star School interpretation sequential arrangement of numbers.

Out of the 216 basic house type charts, this only occurs a few times. It is the type of house an elderly woman would not do well in. Her health fails. It is also a reversed house as described in the previous chapter, which means there can be both money and health problems. All of this information is derived from the house's age in combination with its compass orientation. It is nothing you can see with your naked eyes.

Further, the number combination 4-6 in the center of this house indicates any occupant could have trouble with their low back or legs. Not much of a health area, mistaken by the Black Hat interpretation.

Nor is the master bedroom in the back right-hand corner of the room exactly the marriage corner that the Black Hat School would like you to believe. The 8-1 combination in a bedroom can mean that the husband will be rather monkish and not get enough sex, and that the occupants may suffer from circulation, glandular, ear or kidney problems. Prior to 2004, it can also mean the woman will have betrayals and difficulties.

One of my clients lived in a home such as this and the wife had such a severe case of fibroid myalgia that she was in a constant state of pain. Sex was out of the question for this couple and the husband confided his frustration to me. Putting the metal element in this bedroom would be correct, not the red color (fire), which the Black Hat School and the Compass School would have chosen for different reasons.

CASE STUDY #2

Let's take a look at the exact same floor plan. Let us even say that the house has the exact same compass orientation of facing magnetic northwest at 315 degrees. The only difference with this house is that it was built in 1970 instead of 1950 (see Figure 7-6).

Black Hat School. The interpretation of the house would be the same as their previous impression because they do not know how to factor in the crucial timing and direction.

New Age Compass School. Their interpretation of the house would be the same as the previous example for the same reason.

E 3-9 4	SE 4-8 5	S 9-3 1
NE 8-4 9	C 5-7 6	SW 2-1 3
N 1-2 2	NW 6-6 7	W 7-5 8

Figure 7-6. Flying Star School Chart for 1970 house facing 315 degrees northwest.

Flying Star School. This interpretation would be quite different. This house type is characterized as double-facing—a house that is normally very supportive of financial success. Flying Star practitioners know this house was in a money lock phase from 1984 to 2003, based on information from the facing quadrant of the house. This would help explain why the occupants may have struggled financially, especially in comparison to previous occupants before that particular time frame. The good news is this house is no longer in a bad long-term locked phase.

The 9-3 energy in that master bedroom can contribute to a couple arguing or having legal problems, not exactly an auspicious marriage corner. The good news is that a really smart baby could be conceived in a bedroom with the 9-3 energy.

The energy at the front door (6-6 in the northwest) could reveal that the man in the house is extremely powerful and authoritative, like a police chief, politician or company CEO. But it can also add more fuel to a fighting family.

Hundreds of examples could be given comparing the different schools of feng shui, but I think with just these two comparisons my point is made. Without considering the aspect of timing, the novice or incomplete approach to analyzing a house is incorrect. As a potential feng shui consumer, do you want to have the "one size fits all" analysis or do you want precision and accuracy? If feng shui remedies have the power to work, they also have the power to backfire when placed incorrectly. When you consider the popular (but dumbed-down) Black Hat Map, doesn't it seem absurd for every house to be treated the same?

ANOTHER CONFLICTING THEORY

As illustrated throughout this book, floor plan samples have been given showing how a house is divided into three equal divisions of length and width, producing what are called Lo-shu squares. These square, or rectangular areas—also referred to as quadrants—define the locations of directional zones within a structure. This method is based on the concept that energy has no shape until a space contains it, much like water taking on the shape of its container, and is used by many feng shui masters (see Figure 7-7).

Another method is also used by different schools, whereby the floor plan is divided into directional sectors. These wedge- or pie-shaped sectors begin in the center of the house and fan out like the degrees of a compass. The premise is that the energy starts in the center and emanates like a ray of light projecting straight out (see Figure 7-8). This is another popular method and occasionally there is reason to use one over the other, in my opinion. There are special feng shui applications beyond the scope of this book, where starting from the center of the house and walking a straight line to a certain directional degree identifies the exact proper location for a remedy. You have learned about the construction sha locations, which are located using the sector method.

In comparing the two methods on the same house, the directional areas will land in slightly-to-significantly different areas. If a structure is a perfect square, the directional areas will land in almost the same place. If the structure is rectangular, as shown in Figure 7-8, you can see how some sectors are larger than others when super-imposed over the Lo-shu square method.

This presents a problem in perfecting where to put the appropriate remedy. Using one system, a front door could be located in one direc-

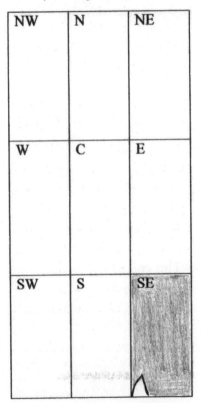

Figure 7-7. A floor plan divided into directional sectors.

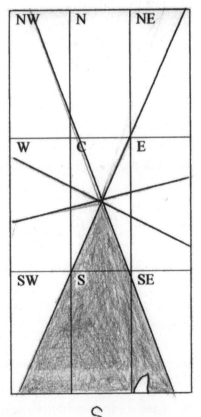

Figure 7-8. Wedge- or pie-shaped sectors to indicate energy emanating from the center.

tion, then deemed a positive or negative entrance. Using the other system may place the front door in another direction with a totally different meaning. In Figure 7-7, the door is in the southeast quadrant. In Figure 7-8, the door is just inside the south sector. Totally different meanings. Both of these methods are rational and plausible to me and proponents of either system will count on their case study evidence to prove their way is the correct way.

The tie breaker for me came in a conversation that I once had with Master Sang. Of all the masters I have studied with, he is the one who is most knowledgeable and experienced in the original branch of feng shui known as Yin House readings. This is the divination of gravesites, which was the first use of feng shui before it was ever applied to homes. He explained to me that using the pie-shaped sectors is reserved for gravesites and is not supposed to be used for Yang House readings. Yang House refers to structures designed for the living. Because I happen to know that some very famous feng shui teachers are mixing up the Yin House material with the Yang House information (teaching techniques for *houses* that are supposed to be for *graves*), I can appreciate that this popular error is real. If you want to study feng shui deeply and be extremely cautious, you may decide to run a continuous comparison of the two systems and track the feedback and results to come to your own conclusions.

CONSUMER TIPS FOR WHAT CONSTITUTES A QUALIFIED PRACTITIONER

Since this chapter is devoted to exposing real feng shui from fake feng shui, it seems appropriate to discuss real feng shui masters versus fake feng shui masters. Or more politely, what does it really take to qualify as a master?

There are four major components that go in to a feng shui reading, and there are four major components that go into becoming a master:

1. *Diplomacy.* A person could have all kinds of technical training and understanding of the mechanics of feng shui, but if they scare all their clients with bad news and insinuate that tragedy is just around the corner, this person cannot be regarded as a feng shui

master in my opinion. The art of dealing with people and behaving like a professional is integral to being a feng shui master because it reflects his or her state of consciousness. Clients are not supposed to sink into a deep depression after a consultation. If their house has problems, they should have been inspired with remedies and solutions. Feng shui practitioners should not have license to behave eccentrically or advise outside the scope of their field unless they make it clear they are doing just that.

Of course, nothing can be done with someone who has a chronically fear-based approach to life. All of my colleagues have experienced the lunacy of gently informing a client about the imperfections of their house, only to have that individual overreact because of their own emotional instability. One time I was advising a woman about her house, and I asked her if her teenage daughters were accident-prone. There were indications that each girl was sleeping in a room with potential to cause injury. She replied they had never had an injury, so I smiled and said, "That's great."

The next day, this woman called to say she couldn't sleep the whole night because I had negatively disposed her to thinking her girls would be in an accident. She also scolded me for getting "too personal" with her. I tried to explain that discussing personal matters is in a feng shui consultant's job description. This is why people call on our services. Additionally, her accusation that I was being "too personal" came out of left field, considering how she literally pulled me aside during the tour of her house, out of earshot of her husband, to tell me she was about to leave him! Often, a feng shui consultant is in a no-win situation because if they forewarn a client about a danger, they are accused of putting negative thoughts into someone's head. Yet if they don't forewarn a person about a problem, their evaluation will later be deemed inaccurate. How would you like it if your doctor knew that you had cancer, but didn't tell you because he didn't want you to worry about it?

This is one instance where the soft-spoken old-time feng shui master gets off easy by saying very little, and not volunteering lengthy explanations to a person from a culture that considers it rude to ask many questions. In comparison, Westerners demand explanations for everything.

2. *Compassion.* People have problems and some want magical cures. They also want to know that their feng shui master is really listening to them. It is impossible for a person to remain in the feng shui business if she does not have compassion for the human race. She will drown in all the sad stories unless she can get personal gratification from helping people find solutions. Helping people is the main goal and a feng shui master will be naturally compassionate even toward the occasional client with unrealistic expectations or demands.

3. *Training.* It is imperative to have a full well-rounded amount of classical training in order to become a feng shui master, otherwise he can just put "Feng Shui Jack of all Trades" on his business card instead. Some folks are deluded or deceived into thinking they have had sufficient training when they haven't. Without exaggeration, some people have been known to start consulting after taking a weekend course. I feel confident however, that as the years progress, this once secretive body of knowledge will become increasingly more available and organized for people who really want to study it. Even people who started out as Black Hat consultants are now pursuing classical feng shui.

4. *Experience.* Once a person has tackled theory training, the next step is to go out and get experience. Training without experience is like a new doctor who has never had any patients. I was once surprised to see an advertisement for a well-known feng shui practitioner who touted that he had more than 600 clients. This was someone who had been in business for 15 years or so. Since I had seen more than 600 clients in my first two years of consulting, it really made me wonder at what point someone can legitimately say he has enough experience to charge for his services and call himself an expert.

I think if a person has been consulting professionally for more than ten years, with a few thousand clients, loads of training and mostly a good track record for helping people, he may feel entitled to call himself a master. Compare this to some lightweight programs from which a student might be granted the title of master after a series of courses and exams, even with little *actual* experience. It reminds me of the old joke, "What do you call a medical student who graduates at the *bottom* of his class?…Doctor."

Experience really is the key. It reminds me how the black belt status in the martial arts system came into being. The martial artist never washed his belt and when it literally turned black, that was an indication of sufficient training and fighting experience. Traditionally, "master" has been a spiritual title that a master teacher personally bestows upon a student, and that would probably be the highest honor.

If you live in a small town or a city where you can't find a local feng shui practitioner to interview, you can consult the Internet where there are more and more practitioners helping people long distance. While it is always better for a consultant to be there in person, an accurate long distance reading can be extremely helpful.

CHAPTER EIGHT

COMMERCIAL USES FOR FENG SHUI

Any structure with four walls and a ceiling can be assessed; it doesn't have to be just a residence. In the majority of feng shui books, the emphasis is on the private residence, but feng shui applications are used just as much for business locations.

DESIGNING OR EVALUATING DIFFERENT BUSINESS TYPES

Here are some basic rules applicable to business:

1. The entrance to a business is critical to its success, especially if clientele or customers need to pass through that entrance as with hotels, yoga centers, supermarkets, etc. Some businesses are not reliant on foot traffic or consumers entering the premises, so the entrance in these cases is not quite so critical. However, the entrance will still affect the health and well-being of the people who work in the building.

2. What is good for the president or owner of the company will have a trickle-down effect on all the employees. In other words, if the president is successful, it usually indicates that the whole company will be successful. This is why the location of the owner's office is so important.

3. The areas where people spend the most time will affect them the most. So the office or work area of a business will be more important than a storage area.

4. Where someone works all day can affect them just as much as where they sleep all night. Where a person works can affect their health, their emotions, their creativity, productivity and success.

5. A good environment for one type of business is not always good for *any* type of business. For example, what might be appropriate for a police station would not necessarily be good feng shui for a furniture store.

What follows are my comments on certain commercial enterprises and what could be "feng shui relevant" to those businesses. This is by no means a complete list, but hopefully will give you some insight that you could extend to businesses not mentioned.

● *Airports.* Aviation is related to the fire element. An airport could be designed with feng shui principles in mind to accommodate the fire element. The design could incorporate features that would help reduce landing accidents and security problems.

● *Amusement parks.* Feng shui could also play a role in the design of an amusement park by noting the location of rides (to avoid malfunctions or accidents), by using the best entrance to draw people in and even the conscious placement of water to enhance the financial potential of the entire park.

● *Animal facilities, zoos and horse ranches.* Animals will succumb to bad feng shui as readily as human beings. Those animals that become sickly, irritated or violent will undoubtedly be in the areas with the same feng shui that would be harmful to a human being.

● *Architectural firms.* Designing is a very creative field and the layout of the architecture office could take into consideration placing the designers in the most creative-inducing areas of the floor plan.

● *Art galleries.* An art gallery will need to draw in people who can appreciate the product being sold. The 4 artistic star should be prominent at this type of location, preferably at the front entrance. I once looked at an art gallery that had recently taken over a space that had been a bookstore for decades. The energy is actually very similar.

Businesses related to art, beauty, fashion, design, music, writing and academia will all need the 4 energy stimulated or used in order to help draw in success. Art studios, libraries, hair salons, spas, performing arts centers and museums can all benefit from a similar feng shui. (The orientation and construction cycle of The Creative House, described in Chapter Five, also applies to commercial properties.)

● *Attorneys' offices.* Those who work regularly with legal documents and legal situations are not in a vulnerable position when working inside structures that attract legal problems. It is their business. This kind of energy can be increased to work in their favor.

● *Auto dealerships.* There is nothing particularly unique about this type of business from a feng shui standpoint, but they do much better when their building has naturally good feng shui and when the cars being sold are in the prosperity areas. Actually, any business or store with inventory can have the placement of the inventory in the most appealing or lucky feng shui areas.

● *Banks and other financial institutions.* Like other businesses, if the building is good, with a good entrance and good areas occupied by the people who do the financial negotiating—then these companies are more likely to succeed. Apparently, most of the banks in Hong Kong have incorporated some feng shui principles in the design and construction phases. Considerations could also be taken to reduce the possibility of robbery.

● *Child care centers.* Children of all ages should be able to learn, play and grow in an environment that supports them. Reducing or eliminating areas that could cause accidents or illness would be a main consideration.

● *Fire stations, hospitals and doctors' offices.* Buildings that deal with emergencies and traumas should take feng shui into consideration in order to help reduce the anxiety of those who work there or enter the premises. At a hospital or doctor's office, the healing can begin right away if the energy of the building is balanced.

● *Golf courses.* Obviously, this is a business that offers a service that takes place outdoors. The success of the golf course will have a lot to do with the lot itself in relation to other businesses, the entrance to the course and the building that houses the golf course's management office.

● *Government buildings.* Most of us have walked through a government building or courthouse at least once and the architecture usually evokes a feeling of seriousness. Some government buildings are beautiful, while others are downright depressing. In order for a government to be powerful, the buildings that house its officials must have strong, positive feng shui.

● *Medical offices.* Most doctors who I have worked with have a two-fold reason for seeking out feng shui advice. They primarily look at their own business just like any other, with a potential for increased financial profits. They almost always want their offices and reception rooms to be balanced and serene for the sake of their patients. This is so that patients will feel comfortable while waiting for treatment and have an all-round positive experience, with a desire to return.

● *Mortuaries and cemeteries.* The mortuary itself is similar to other businesses in that there is money to be made and a desire for a good reputation within the community. Although occasionally a mortuary achieves notoriety in the press by mishandling their deceased or doing something undignified or illegal.

The very first applications of feng shui were used specifically for the proper site of graves. It is referred to as Yin House readings and is taken very seriously by many Asian families. To ensure receiving good luck and a prosperous future, people must make sure their loved ones have been buried in a cemetery plot that has good feng shui. What constitutes good feng shui for a grave is similar to good feng shui for a house, although there are some distinctions that are only relevant to the grave. This is a whole separate branch of feng shui to which few Westerners have been exposed. It is not even possible to practice Yin House (gravesite) readings without the combined knowledge of both Flying Star and Form Schools.

● *Prisons.* If I were involved in the design phase of a prison, I would explicitly try to avoid having prison cells located in areas prone to arguments or violence. I would also recommend other design and décor features to help inmates stay relaxed. This is not just for their benefit (since they are there to be punished), but for the benefit of the people who work at these tension-filled, dangerous institutions.

● *Religious facilities.* Any house of worship will have characteristics unique to the people who use the space and their religious beliefs. Master Sang made reference to the difference between a Buddhist temple and a Taoist temple, in that the Buddhist temple would traditionally need to be more yang, and the Taoist temple more yin, consistent with the differences in how these sects worship and their distinct beliefs. The central energy of a religious center will convey the potential effect on or attitude of the congregation. We all know religious institutions are not immune to legal, ethical and political scandals.

● *Restaurants.* The location of the kitchen is the most important part of a restaurant; the product is created in this location so the food will resonate with the good or bad feng shui. This is a similar concept to the fact that a cook's own hands can instill good or bad energy into the food. The location of the entrance is the second-most important area and the location of the cash register is the third most important area. To help ensure success, these three areas should all be in the best quadrants of the building.

If the restaurant has a bar, it is actually okay for the bar to be in a relatively negative area. What often draws people to drink alcohol is their loneliness or unhappiness and a strategically placed bar can stimulate those emotions. This is just one example of taking something negative and turning it into something profitable for a business.

● *Schools, colleges and universities* All educational buildings should be environments conducive to studying and excelling. If feng shui were used right in the design phase, the entire plot plan could be broken down in to the best areas for buildings versus outside space. Then each building could be analyzed on its own merit and each classroom could have an ideal arrangement. There would naturally be some buildings better for science versus the arts. Even the shapes of the buildings could help accentuate the type of learning going on inside.

● *Shopping centers.* Since every structure will have some negative zones, it is impossible for every store in a shopping center to have good feng shui. The only way to compensate is within the interiors of each store, giving them the best possible individual door, cash register location, inventory placement, and the most attractive design features including lighting.

There is so much emphasis on peace and serenity in the home, but for businesses a little chaos can be good. Just like going to a good garage sale where we don't mind foraging through piles to find a hidden treasure, the psychological triggers to shopping and spending could be called subliminal feng shui.

This is where wild colors, flashing lights, hard surfaces, loud music, the smell of food and fragrances can all be used to make us think less rationally and more emotionally. Some companies have their own brand of subliminal feng shui down to a real marketing science.

The list could go on regarding all the possibilities for commercial uses of feng shui. I have always found a direct correlation between any type of business doing well or poorly and the most basic feng shui features. The skeptic might think of it as coincidence, but my experience tells me otherwise.

Years ago I went to look at a Mobil gas station, which also had an auto repair shop attached to it, plus a car wash, a McDonald's restaurant and a mini-mart. It was all in one big compound. Without knowing anything about these businesses, I was able to identify (through calculations) that the car wash was in the best prosperity area and the McDonald's restaurant was in an area that could cause legal problems. The owner divulged that the car wash did better than any other business in the compound and the McDonald's was about to sue the mini-mart for selling coffee, which violated their previous agreement not to compete with each other with food and beverages.

Over and over again, I receive feedback from landlords and owners that the perpetually hard-to-lease retail spaces, the spaces with the highest turnover or the problem tenants are always in the negative feng shui areas.

Whether it's a pet store, a gambling casino, a drug rehabilitation center or a jeans manufacturing plant, any structure can be diagnosed according to these universal theories.

CHAPTER NINE

KIDS, DON'T TRY THIS AT HOME

I hope this book has peaked your interest in learning more about feng shui. I hope it has answered many of your questions about how a comprehensive analysis is done, as well as some particulars about your own personal space.

You are not expected to digest all the information the first time around and you may want to read the book again and practice with some of the formulas. I highly recommend doing that because the only way to really solidify what you have learned is through repetition. For ease in analyzing your own home or business, you should make a transparency of one of the compass Illustrations so that you can lay it over your floor plan to determine where certain important directions are, once you have taken an actual compass reading. By doing this, you can always identify the construction sha areas to avoid or remedy in any given year. A good quality compass can be found at a camping or sporting goods store, as well as other locations.

And if you proceed to study more feng shui, you will have already prepared an accurate depiction of your floor plan.

The more one studies feng shui, the more questions crop up. They seem endless. There will be other authors and books you can refer to for the entire 216 basic charts, and there will probably be a software program available after this book is published.

If you choose to study with a competent teacher or classical school, you can find out how to do the calculations by hand and learn the intricacies of all the number combinations and their meanings.

Most people do not want to study feng shui deeply and they should seriously consider hiring a professional. In the same way that you can read a nutrition book and receive some good information, you should still see a doctor if you have a serious problem.

Please consider this book an invitation to any reader who needs clarification on something discussed in its chapters or who wants to ask further questions. Feel free to contact me via my website and join my monthly newsletter. If you want either local or long distance feng shui advice, I am here to help, and will probably never retire.

—*Kartar Diamond*
www.fengshuisolutions.net
www.kartardiamond.com

ABOUT THE AUTHOR

Kartar Diamond grew up in South- ern California in the 1970s and always had a fascination with metaphysical top- ics. She has also had an enduring interest in holistic lifestyle choices and studying how people are affected by their environ- ment.

In 1992, a chance meeting with Grand Master Sang began Kartar's for- mal feng shui studies. She has since become one of his best-known certified graduates and instructors. Sang's school, the American Feng Shui Institute, enjoys a worldwide reputation as one of the most comprehensive classical feng shui learning centers.

In 1993, Kartar launched her own consulting business, Feng Shui Solutions, and routinely works with several hundred clients per year. Kartar advises on both existing residential and commercial properties in addition to house-hunting and design phase projects.

Kartar teaches introductory classes at numerous state colleges and adult schools and came out with her own Traditional Video Workshop Series in 1999.

Her professional alliances have included the American Society of Interior Designers and she is referred to by many real estate companies including Coldwell Banker.

Kartar's lengthy list of speaking engagements has included Barnes & Noble Booksellers, Universal Studios, Xerox Corporation, the Los Angeles Country Club, and USC's Festival of Health, to name a few.

Feng Shui for Skeptics: Real Solutions Without Superstition, is a manifestation of having studied every branch and style of feng shui, voluminous hands-on experience and case study feedback, as well as a passion for educating the Western world about the benefits of this greatly unknown and misunderstood ancient practice.

Her book stands out for its uniqueness in being able to deliver advanced information in a user-friendly format, prioritize the most important things for readers and consumers to be aware of, as well as for dispelling the myths and superstitions that cloud the integrity of feng shui as a legitimate earth science and healing art.

Kartar's future will undoubtedly include the publishing of more educational materials and delivering this time-honored wisdom to the people who need it most.

Kartar's second book,
The Feng Shui Matrix: Another Way to Inherit the Earth,
will be published in 2006.
If you would like to be notified when the book is available,
email us at info@FourPillarsPublishing.com.

Give the Gift of
FENG SHUI
FOR
SKEPTICS
to Your Friends and Colleagues

CHECK YOUR LEADING BOOKSTORE OR ORDER HERE

❑ **YES**, I want _____ copies of *Feng Shui for Skeptics* at $14.95 each, plus $4.95 shipping per book (CA residents please add $1.23 sales tax per book). Canadian orders must be accompanied by a postal money order in U.S. funds. Allow 15 days for delivery.

❑ **YES**, I am interested in having Kartar Diamond speak or give a seminar to my company, association, school, or organization. Please send information.

❑ **For a comprehensive consultation** on your property contact Kartar at 310-842-8870 or e-mail her at Kartar@fengshuisolutions.net.

My check or money order for $_____ is enclosed.

Please charge my   ❑ Visa   ❑ MasterCard

Name _____

Organization _____

Address _____

City/State/Zip _____

Phone_____ E-mail_____

Card _____

Exp. Date_____ Signature _____

Please make your check payable and return to:
Four Pillars Publishing
3824 Perham Drive • Culver City, CA 90232
Call your credit card order to: 310-842-8870
Fax: 310-842-8914